The Encyclopedia of
GREETING CARD
Tools & Techniques

The Encyclopedia of
GREETING CARD
Tools & Techniques

Susan Pickering Rothamel

LARK BOOKS

A Division of Sterling Publishing Co., Inc.
New York / London

Senior Editor: **Ray Hemachandra**

Editor: **Larry Shea**

Assistant Editors: **Mark Bloom and Cassie Moore**

Art Director: **Kathleen Holmes**

Assistant Art Director: **Avery Johnson**

Photographers: **Stewart O'Shields and Shawn Hall**

Cover Designer: **Cindy LaBreacht**

Library of Congress Cataloging-in-Publication Data

Rothamel, Susan Pickering.
      Encyclopedia of greeting cards tools and techniques   /   Susan Pickering Rothamel.—1st ed.
          p. cm.
      Includes index.
      ISBN-13: 978-1-60059-029-0 (hc-plc with jacket : alk. paper)
      ISBN-10: 1-60059-029-2 (hc-plc with jacket : alk. paper)
      1.   Greeting cards.   2. Handicraft.   I.   Title.
    TT872.R67 2008
    745.594'1--dc22
                     2007050641

10 9 8 7 6 5 4 3

Published by Lark Books, A Division of Sterling Publishing Co., Inc.
387 Park Avenue South, New York, NY 10016

Text and illustrations © 2008, Susan Pickering Rothamel
Photography © 2008, Lark Books unless otherwise specified

Distributed in Canada by Sterling Publishing, c/o Canadian Manda Group, 165 Dufferin Street
Toronto, Ontario, Canada M6K 3H6

Distributed in the United Kingdom by GMC Distribution Services,
Castle Place, 166 High Street, Lewes, East Sussex, England BN7 1XU

Distributed in Australia by Capricorn Link (Australia) Pty Ltd.,
P.O. Box 704, Windsor, NSW 2756 Australia

If you have questions or comments about this book, please contact:
Lark Books
67 Broadway
Asheville, NC 28801
828-253-0467

Manufactured in China

ISBN 13: 978-1-60059-029-0

For information about custom editions, special sales, and premium and corporate purchases, please contact the Sterling Special Sales Department at 800-805-5489 or specialsales@sterlingpub.com.

Contents

Introduction

THIS BOOK is a true labor of love. My goal was to gather together all the history, terminology, how-to advice, and inspiration you need to appreciate the great tradition of making and sending cards and to become a cardmaker yourself. The timeline that starts off the book covers everything from the first Valentine in 270 AD to the most recent developments in the greeting-card industry. The alphabetical journey that follows defines and explains techniques (*Dry Embossing* and *Gilding*, for example), tools (*Corrugator, Stylus*), types of cards (*Fold-Out, Repurposed*), and much more. Many of the entries include a "How-to Basics" section that teaches you how the techniques are actually done. Examples of contemporary and historical cards add explanation and inspiration to the topics covered.

For many people, collecting the mail is just another routine task in a busy day. But imagine leafing through the bills, advertisements, and credit-card solicitations only to find a square white envelope. Your name is handwritten on it, and there's a real postage stamp in the upper right-hand corner. Anticipation mounting, you pause and say to yourself, "Wow, someone sent me a card!"

Sending a card is almost as nice as receiving one. In truth, I used to wonder if my family and friends really appreciated my handmade cards. But the few times I've sent store-bought cards, they've been quick to ask if everything is okay, as if getting an ordinary card from me means something is wrong. It's a nice feeling to know that they attach value to my humble gifts.

As you'll discover in this book, handmade cards have a long and admirable history. Today, unfortunately, many people think of greeting cards only as what they see in those racks at the local drugstore. Over the years, making cards has been transformed from an individual, relatively rare pursuit into a big business. There are approximately 3,000 card publishers in the United States alone. Americans purchase nearly seven billion greeting cards every year, generating nearly $7.5 billion in retail sales.

With today's rising interest in paper crafts of all types, more and more people are bringing the greeting card back to its origins as a unique item designed to express truly personal sentiments. The craft industry provides an abundance of paper materials and a myriad of cardmaking embellishments, from ribbons and beads to stickers and rubberstamps. An amazing array of materials is available. You only need to look for a large craft store, an independent

paper shop, or even your local grocery store. Today, anyone can create a greeting card from the comfort of home.

You'll be astounded by the hundreds of creative cards displayed in this book. I can't begin to thank all of the artists who kindly allowed me to share their cards. Some cardmakers are enthusiastic crafters who just enjoy the cardmaking process and use fairly traditional materials. Others are fabulous designers and artists who labor over each card, developing special techniques and carefully composing their color schemes.

A number of these cardmakers are featured in the artist profiles sprinkled throughout the book. You'll meet Dee Gruenig, a multi-talented cardmaker, instructor, and entrepreneur who truly can be considered the "Queen of Stamping," as well as Cy Thiewes, an artist who was inspired in her retirement to recycle her watercolor paintings into brilliantly vibrant cards. All of the artists whose work you'll see here are proudly carrying on the centuries-old tradition of handmade cards.

Traditions are meant to be passed along. I hope that the words and images that follow inspire you to join in the tradition yourself—or, if you're already a seasoned cardmaker, to expand your horizons and try out some of the many enticing methods for creating cards you'll find here.

Most of the designs in the book are relatively easy to produce right at your own kitchen table. Use what you have at hand, such as pressed leaves and flowers, scrapbooking materials, computer paper, and rubberstamps. If you are a fine artist, think "off the wall" and consider the card stock as your canvas. Adapt your more formal art supplies, and use them to start your own cardmaking tradition.

The soup-to-nuts information—actually, *Accordion Fold* to *Wrinkling*—you'll find in this encyclopedia will help you begin and provide hundreds of ideas to inspire your creativity. Making your own cards is extremely satisfying, and one day you may see your work framed on a friend's wall or saved in a scrapbook album. If so, you'll know your gift—a humble, heartfelt handmade card—will be treasured forever.

The History of Greeting Cards

A Sumerian tablet

BC

Sumerians invent cuneiform writing. Using a blunt reed to make cuneiform ("wedge-shaped") impressions on clay tablets, they attain both a method of record keeping and a message delivery system.

2000–2500 BC

The Egyptians invent hieroglyphics and papyrus, a paper-like substance, which allows them to convey messages and greetings much easier than using clay tablets.

1500–1000 BC

The Aztecs paint intricate designs on prepared bark. These petroglyph messages are carried by runners to recipients.

600 BC

The Greeks develop long scrolls of parchment made of goat skin, which is more durable than papyrus.

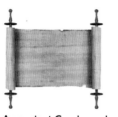

An ancient Greek parchment

105 AD

China produces an economical paper made of a variety of materials. Can greeting cards be far behind?

270

According to legend, St. Valentine, a third-century Roman priest, performs secret marriages against the order of Emperor Claudius II. The Emperor, who believes single soldiers are more likely to join his army, has Valentine arrested. Before his execution on February 14, the priest sends a note to the jailer's daughter, signing it "From Your Valentine."

496

Pope Gelasius authorizes February 14 to honor St. Valentine as the patron saint of lovers. According to the *Catholic Encyclopedia*, there are at least three early Christian saints by that name: the priest in Rome, a bishop in Terni, and a missionary in Africa. According the the book, the three die or are martyred on February 14.

500–1000

Western cultures still copy books by hand onto animal skin parchment. The process is too long and costly for greeting cards.

593

China invents the first printing press.

600–750

Greeting cards make another evolutionary step forward when papermaking techniques spread throughout Asia and the Middle East. The Japanese refine the art.

901

The Chinese use wood blocks to print pictures and text. The Japanese begin the art form of origami, linking it with their message-sending tradition.

1238

Spain develops the first paper mills, but not the first greeting cards.

1400s

Handmade paper greeting cards are exchanged in Europe. Germans print seasonal New Year's greetings called Andachtsbilder from woodcuts. A devotional picture, most often decorated with the Christ Child, includes the sentiment "A good and blessed year."

1415

The first written valentine may have come from Charles, Duke of Orleans, who wrote romantic verses to his wife while imprisoned.

1420

John Lydgate composes a Valentine's Day greeting for Henry V to give to Catherine of Valois:

> Seynte Valentine of custome yeere by yeere
> Men have an usance, in this regioun
> To loke and serche Cupides kalendar,
> And chose theyr choyse by grete affeccioun,
> Such has been move with Cupides nocioun,
> Takying theyre choyse as theyre sort doth falle;
> But I love oon whiche excelleth alle.

1450

In Europe, Johann Gutenberg invents the first printing press with movable type, which allows him to economically print many copies of the Bible.

1470

Woodcuts are introduced in Europe to illustrate the printed word.

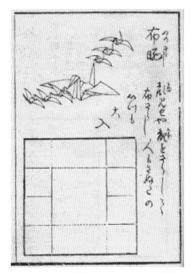

A page from *Hiden Senbazuru Orikata*, the oldest origami book in the world, ca. 1797

A German woodcut from an Andachtsbilder

The 1450 Gutenberg press

1476

William Caxton becomes the first printer in Westminster, England.

1477

Margery Brews sends her fiancé a Valentine Card. It is the oldest known greeting card still in existence. Here is a portion:

> *Unto my ryght welebelovyd Voluntyn, John Paston, Squyer, be this bill delyvered, &c.*
> Ryght reverent and wurschypfull, and my ryght welebeloved Volutyne,
> I recomande me unto yowe, ffull hertely desyring to here of yowr welefare,
> whech I beseche Almyghty God long for to preserve un to Hys plesur,
> and yowr herts desyre. And yf it please yowe to here of my welefar,
> I am not in good heele of body, nor of herte, nor schall be tyll I her ffrom yowe;
> For there wottys no creature what peyn that I endure,
> And for to be deede, I dare it not dyscure [discover].

1500

European presses begin printing books.

GREETING CARD FUN FACTS

U.S. consumers purchase approximately seven billion greeting cards each year, generating nearly $7.5 billion in retail sales.

More than 90 percent of all U.S. households buy greeting cards, with the average household purchasing 30 individual cards in a year.

In 1954, Americans sent about two billion Christmas cards. Today, the yearly figure stands at close to four billion, or an average of 20 cards per person.

Sixty-two percent of people feel inspired to send someone a card if they have received one from that person.

Women purchase more than 80 percent of all greeting cards.

Women are more likely than men to buy several cards at once. However, men generally spend more on a single card.

The two categories of greeting cards are seasonal and everyday. Sales are split approximately 50-50 between the two types.

The most popular seasonal cards are Christmas (60 percent), Valentine's Day (25 percent), Mother's Day (4 percent), Easter (3 percent), and Father's Day (3 percent).

The most popular everyday cards are birthday (60 percent), anniversary (8 percent), get well (7 percent), friendship (6 percent), and sympathy cards (6 percent).

There are an estimated 3,000 greeting card publishers in the U.S. alone.

The United Kingdom is the world leader in sending greetings cards, spending more than £1 billion each year.

Until Christmas 1961, the UK Post Office used to deliver cards on Christmas morning.

Among industrialized countries, the average person receives more than 20 cards per year, about one-third of which are birthday cards.

Source: *Some of the above facts are courtesy of the Greeting Card Association (www.greetingcard.org).*

1639

The Boston, Massachusetts, tavern of Richard Fairbanks, becomes the first repository for overseas mail.

1775

New Year's, Valentine's Day, and Christmas cards become popular. Commercially made, they feature mechanical, pop-up, and filigree effects.

On July 26, members of the Second Continental Congress agree "... that a Postmaster General be appointed for the United States, and be paid a salary of 1,000 dollars per year." Benjamin Franklin becomes the first Postmaster General under the Continental Congress.

1789

Mass-produced Valentine's Day cards become available.

Samuel Osgood becomes the first Postmaster General under the U.S. Constitution.

1796

Johann Nepomuk Franz Alois Senefelder of Prague, Czechoslovakia, perfects a chemical printing process the French dub "lithography." Within 25 years, European printers are mass-producing lithographed devotional prints. By 1825, the new technology is common in the United States. By the 1840s, Senefelder's color process—known as "chromolithography"—gives an added dimension to small die-cuts and greeting cards.

Johann Nepomuk Franz Alois Senefelder, inventer of lithography

1825

The U.S. 'dead letter' office is formed.

1829

The U.S. Postmaster General, William T. Barry of Kentucky, joins Andrew Jackson's President's Cabinet.

1830s

Esther Howland, known as the Mother of the Valentine, makes fancy Valentines with real lace, ribbons, and colorful pictures known as "scrap."

Esther sent ten prototype designs to her brother, a salesman for a stationery company. The response was enormous—in New England alone, he took orders for over $5000. Esther purchased color pictures, paper lace, and real ribbon. Recruiting her friends, she set up an assembly line: one cut pictures, another adhered flowers, and a third attached ribbon or lace. Artisans painted floral elements on silk—sometimes adding a small mirror—as embellishments.

Sold for fifty cents, each Valentine was a fantasy of romance and inspiration. No one could compete with Esther's style or quality. She was among the first entrepreneurs to recognize the potential of assembly-line production. Her business showed profits of $100,000 each year, amazing considering the era. When Whitney Company bought her card line and began machine-producing the cards, Esther's intricate, handmade designs became a thing of the past.

One of Esther Howland's original Valentine's Day cards

1837

Sir Rowland Hill, Postmaster General of England, proposes reformation of the postal system, including a set rate for postage to be paid by the sender.

1838

U.S. Congress designates railroad postal routes.

1840

Queen Victoria begins sending Christmas cards.

May 1: The world's first postage stamp with an adhesive on the back is issued. Sir Henry Cole designs the black-and-white one-cent stamp with a portrait of Queen Victoria, nicknamed the "Penny Black." It is quickly replaced by the Penny Red because the Postal Service could not distinguish the black cancellation ink over the black stamp. On May 8, a two-penny blue stamp becomes available.

1843

The 1843 Horsley card, courtesy of Hallmark Archives, Hallmark Cards, Inc. John Calcott Horsley became the world's first Christmas card sender when he presented Sir Henry Cole with a signed copy of his original design, bearing the inscription:

> "To his good friend Cole
> Who's a merry young soul
> And a merry young soul is he:
> And may he be for many years to come! Hooray!"

Sir Henry Cole hires artist John Calcott Horsley to design a holiday card for friends and acquaintances. The card is also sold commercially for one shilling each. Since it depicts a family with a small child drinking wine together, some critics claim the card encourages intemperance. About 1,000 cards are printed in black and white and then hand-colored. Originals are extremely rare—only about ten have survived—but you can easily find the 1955 reprints.

1847

July 1: In New York City, the first postage stamps are issued in the United States. The first five-cent stamp depicting Benjamin Franklin and the ten-cent George Washington are released.

1848

The first public mailboxes appear in Russia on December 13. Made of wood and iron, they are often stolen. Future mailboxes are made of cast iron, weighing about 88 pounds (40 kilos). Greeting cards are finally safe.

1851

The earliest American-made Christmas cards are store advertisements by R.H. Pease Great Variety in Albany, New York. The lithograph card depicts Santa Claus with a family enjoying their presents, while a servant sets the table. In subsequent years, the cards show mangers, holly, snowmen, and even Little Red Riding Hood.

1852

Pre-stamped envelopes are introduced. A two-cent stamp in black featuring Andrew Jackson is issued. It is dubbed the "Black Jack."

1854

Perforated stamps are introduced.

1856

Louis Prang becomes known as the Father of the Christmas Card, producing cards at his Boston lithographic shop every year for the holiday.

1860

The four-color, photo-mechanical lithographic printing process evolves. This process revolutionizes the printing industry, providing speedy, cost-effective card printing.

1860s

Charles Bennett, Goodall, and Marcus Ward & Co. begin mass-producing greeting cards.

The US Pony Express is introduced.

1863

The US Postal service unifies postage rates, regardless of distance or pages.

1868

Kate Greenaway designs greeting cards for Marcus Ward. Her subjects consist of children, flowers, and landscapes.

1870

Victorians collect beautifully printed cards and scraps for their parlor albums. Trade cards, issued by businesses to advertise their products, become highly collectible.

1872

The first advertising postcard appears in England.

1873

United States Postal Service begins issuing pre-stamped one-cent post cards.

1875

Louis Prang, a German immigrant, publishes the first line of U.S. Christmas cards.

1881

John Calcott Horsley popularizes Christmas cards.

1889

The Heligoland card is considered the first multi-colored postcard ever printed.

A Louis Prang Christmas card from the 1870s, courtesy of Hallmark Archives, Hallmark Cards, Inc.

An 1868 Kate Greenaway Christmas card, courtesy of Dwayne Hill. www.kategreenawaycards.com

A trade card from the Woolson Spice Co., from the collection of Susan Pickering Rothamel

An 1895 "Little Girl" postcard from the collection of Susan Pickering Rothamel

The 1905 Sapirstein logo

A 1906 Ellen H. Clapsaddle postcard from the collection of Susan Pickering Rothamel

1891

In Norfolk, Nebraska, brothers Rollie and William Hall buy the Norfolk Post Card Company bookstore. In 1894, they begin selling postcards wholesale.

1893

The first commemorative U.S. postage stamps are introduced.

1898

Congress ends the U.S. Postal Service's monopoly for printing postcards, passing the Private Mailing Card Act. The new law allows private publishers and printers to produce postcards to be mailed for one cent (the same rate as government postcards), instead of two cents. This was perhaps the most important event in making the cards more popular.

Postcards still have an "undivided back." Writing is allowed only on the front side of the card.

Early 1900s

"Real Photo" postcards are introduced, on film stock paper. While most "Real Photo" postcards are advertising and trade cards, many depict entertainers and portraits of family members.

1901

On December 24, the U.S. begins using the words "Post Card" on the back of the card and writing is still only allowed on the front.

1902

England begins printing divided-back postcards.

1905

Jacob Sapirstein, a young Polish immigrant, arrives in Cleveland, Ohio. He borrows $50 to buy German penny postcards, selling them to drug stores, novelty shops, and confectioners. His sons Irving, Morris, and Harry—as well as his daughter Bernice—help organize inventory, stuff fancy postcards into envelopes, and make deliveries to accounts.

1906

Eastman Kodak enters the marketplace with photo and lithographed greeting cards.

Ellen H. Clapsaddle's artwork is published by the Wolf Company, an outlet for the International Art Company. According to the Greeting Card Association, Clapsaddle is a pioneer and considered the most prolific of all postcard and greeting card artists. Sadly, Clapsaddle died unknown and penniless the day before her 69th birthday.

1907

On March 1, the U.S. allows messages to be written on the back of postcards.

1910

Eighteen-year-old Joyce Hall (b. 1891) moves to Kansas City, Missouri—the future home of the Hallmark Greeting Card Company. Joyce wholesales postcards from his YMCA room until complaints about the large volume of mail convince him to rent an office.

1911

Hall Brothers is formed when Joyce's brother Rollie moves to Kansas City.

Airmail begins between Garden City and Mineola, NY. Earle H. Ovington becomes known as the first U.S. mail pilot.

1912

The Halls add greeting cards to their line as the popularity of postcards begins to decline.

1914

President Woodrow Wilson signs a Congressional resolution declaring, "The American mother is the greatest source of the country's strength and inspiration." He sets the second Sunday in May as the official "Mother's Day."

Government-owned and -operated postal vehicles begin service.

1915

The Hall Brothers begin imprinting their name on their cards. Rollie Hall recognizes the potential in high-quality Valentine's Day and Christmas cards, mailed in envelopes, and begins to create and print such cards. In January, however, a fire destroys the Hall Brothers' office as well as their entire inventory, including all unfilled Valentine orders.

1916

Postal inspectors solve the last known stagecoach robbery.

1917

Hall Brothers launches their first humorous greeting cards. The company is a success. J.C. Hall begins Hall Brother's first foray into other product lines, inventing modern gift wrap.

1918

In an epidemic that kills 20 million people worldwide, influenza (or simply, "the flu") hits America. Jacob Sapirstein is bedridden, and his son Irving, only 9 years old, delivers the Sapirstein Greeting Card Christmas and Valentine's Day card orders. By age 12, he is keeping the company books.

An early private mailing card from the collection of Susan Pickering Rothamel

An early greeting card from the collection of Susan Pickering Rothamel

A Valentine's Day card produced during World War II, from the collection of Susan Pickering Rothamel

A 1928 *Ladies' Home Journal* **advertisement for Hallmark Christmas cards**

An early "pop-up" Valentine's Day card, used with permission from the Moore Collection, Houston, Texas

1920

First transcontinental airmail is delivered.

1924

President Calvin Coolidge recommends that Father's Day be observed throughout the U.S.

Regular transcontinental airmail service begins.

1925

The typeset word "Hallmark" appears on products for the first time, but "Hall Brothers" still is more dominant and appears on most cards.

1927

Calvin Coolidge sends the first White House Christmas card.

International airmail begins.

1928

The typeset word "Hallmark" now appears on the back of every greeting card. Hallmark advertisements appear for the first time in *Ladies' Home Journal*.

1929

American Greetings introduces the first self-serve greeting card display fixtures. Prior to this, shoppers had to flip through an album and then ask a shopkeeper to pull the card from behind the counter.

1931

Canadian company W.E. Coutts Co. becomes an affiliate of Hall Brothers, becoming its first international venture.

1932

In the first licensing venture for both companies, Disney characters appear on Hallmark greeting cards for the first time.

1939

Hallmark's best-selling "Pansy" Mother's Day greeting card (originally five cents each) sells 30 million copies.

Trans-Atlantic airmail begins.

1941

The Greeting Card Association is formed in the United States, under the leadership of George Burkhardt, of Burkhardt-Warner Publishers. The formation of it is a response to a War Department order during World War II to reduce paper use by 25 percent.

1942

The Greeting Card Association begins the "Greeting Cards in Wartime" program. Distributing cards by the Red Cross to wounded servicemen, the program's purpose is to help families keep in touch and boost the morale of soldiers fighting abroad.

V-mail begins. A system for delivering mail from United States troops stationed abroad during World War II, V-mail worked by photographing large amounts of censored mail onto reels of film. The reels were then shipped to the U.S. and printed out on lightweight photo paper, to then be delivered to the addressees.

The 1939 "Pansy" card, reproduced with permission from Hallmark Corporation

On the cover: "To let you know I'm thinking of you." **Inside:** "Pansies always stand for thoughts—at least that's what folks say. So this just comes to show my thoughts are there with you today."

A V-Mail greeting card from the collection of Susan Pickering Rothamel

A greeting card from home, reproduced with permission from American Greetings Corporation.

A greeting card from a soldier, from the collection of Susan Pickering Rothamel

The Hallmark logo, reproduced with permission from Hallmark Corporation

Hallmark Cards, Inc.
World Headquarters, Kansas City, Missouri, 2007
Courtesy of Hallmark Corporation

IT'S YOUR BIRTHDAY, AND WOULD YOU BELIEVE IT, YOU STILL LOOK LIKE A MILLION BUCKS!

An early "Hi Brow" card, reproduced with permission from American Greetings Corporation.

1943
Postal zoning is recognized by 124 major post offices.

1944
Hallmark begins using the slogan "When You Care Enough to Send the Very Best."

1945
Caspari, Inc., of New York City, begins producing products inspired by museum collections from the Musée de l'Impression sur Étoffes, The National Gallery of Williamsburg, and The Royal Horticultural Society, as well as private collections. Caspari also imports and sells Christmas cards by European artists.

1949
Andrew Szoeke, a renowned lettering artist and designer from New York, creates the familiar Hallmark logo.

1950
Studio cards with cartoon illustrations and occasional risque humor appear. Building on the "beatnik" anti-establishment and counterculture momentum, American Greetings launches a new irreverent and witty type of greeting card called "Hi Brows."

1952
Sapirstein Greeting Cards becomes the American Greetings Corporation, a publicly held company.

1959
Hallmark introduces Ambassador Cards, launched to serve mass-distribution markets.

1960
Small but highly creative card companies, many launched with very little capital, begin to influence the card market, generating sales throughout the world.

Facsimile (fax) mail begins.

1963
ZIP codes are introduced.

1964
Self-service post offices appear.

1967

American Greetings debuts Holly Hobby, the first licensed property launched by Those Characters from Cleveland, Inc. (TCFC, Inc.), an American Greetings subsidiary. From this come other licensed characters, such as Strawberry Shortcake, Care Bears, and the Get Along Gang.

1968

Priority Mail, a subclass of First-Class Mail, is introduced.

1970

Express Mail begins on an experimental basis.

1971

The United States Postal Service (U.S.P.S.) begins. The Postmaster General is no longer a Cabinet position.

1972

Postage stamps become available by U.S. mail.

1980

New postal standards require envelopes and postcards to be at least 3½ inches (8.9 cm) high and 5 inches (12.7 cm) long.

Greeting card manufacturers develop a three-dimensional card—uniquely presented as the gift itself—that can be sent flat through the mail.

1983

ZIP + 4 is introduced.

The American Greetings logo, courtesy of American Greetings Corporation.

A vintage greeting card, used with permission from the Moore Collection, Houston, Texas

AMERICAN GREETINGS

American Greetings' new "Rose Logo," courtesy of American Greeting Card Co.

1985

American Greetings acquires Dallas-based Drawing Board Greetings, Inc. The acquired company later becomes Carlton Cards, Inc., USA.

1986

At the age of 101, Jacob Sapirstein celebrates the Silver Anniversary of American Greetings by unveiling the "Rose Logo" as part of its corporate identity.

1988

The Greeting Card Association initiates the Louie Awards to celebrate creative excellence in the greeting card industry. Entries are judged on a ten-point scale for criteria that include Imagination, Impact, Artistry, Harmony, Sendability, and Value, with cards in each category divided by price.

1992

Stamps are now sold through automatic teller machines.

GREETING CARD TIPS

Make sending a card or two a weekly habit instead of an occasional afterthought.

While e-cards are easy to send, they rarely reach the heart of their recipient. Take the time to send the real thing.

Personalize the message. Even if a sentiment is pre-printed, add your own words at the bottom or a longer note on the inside.

Always date your cards so that future generations will know the month and year treasured cards were sent.

Instead of using address labels and metered postage, use a stamp and handwrite—or even use an old-fashioned typewriter to type—the address on the envelope.

When complimenting someone for a job well done, sending congratulations, or just saying "I'm thinking of you," be specific and tell the person exactly why you're sending a card. ("Congratulations! Your patients are going to have the best care with you as their nurse.")

Always sign the card, even if your name is printed.

Keep your signature informal—no titles for business associates and no last names for family or friends.

Include your return address. Doing so not only complies with postal service regulations, but also helps your friends keep their mailing lists up-to-date.

Don't wait for a special occasion or a reason to connect. Send an unexpected card for no particular reason. A "thinking of you" or "just because" card can be one of the best ways to show someone you care.

1994

Hallmark invests in Aesop, a domestic Japanese stationary manufacturer. (In 1997, Hallmark increases its share in the company up to 100 percent. In the same year there is a name change, to Nihon Hallmark.)

The card most often sent in Japan is the New Year's greeting card. Next in popularity is the summer greeting card, sent to say "Best wishes" to the recipient. People send dozens of cards to friends and family, handwriting a message.

Hallmark's artist Gary Head at work, courtesy of Hallmark Cards, Inc.

1996

American Greetings launches its site on the World Wide Web, featuring paper greeting cards, electronic cards, candy, flowers, and gifts, including Egreetings.com and BlueMountain.com.

2000

Gibson joins American Greetings, combining the world's two largest publicly held greeting card companies.

2007

May 14: After increasing the rate 13 times in 32 years, the U.S. Postal Service introduces a 42-cent first-class stamp.

The U.S. Postal Service introduces "The Forever Stamp." On sale on April 12 at 41 cents, customers can begin using it on May 14. Even if the price of postage should increase, the Forever Stamp can be used without additional postage.

The American Greetings Corporation World Headquarters, Cleveland, Ohio, 2007. Reproduced with permission from American Greetings Corporation

On August 8, AmericanGreetings.com launches a Web-to-Mobile greeting card service in the U.S. This new technology enables e-cards to be delivered to cell phones.

AUTHOR'S NOTE

With appreciation, I wish to thank these companies and organizations for their enormous cooperation in providing much of the valuable information contained in this timeline, as well as providing, or granting the rights to reproduce, many of these historical photographs.

American Greetings
www.americangreetings.com

Hallmark
www.hallmark.com

United States Postal Service
www.usps.com

ACCORDION FOLDING

A card making technique where each fold runs in the opposite direction to the previous fold, creating a pleated or fanlike effect. *See also* Fold-Out Card.

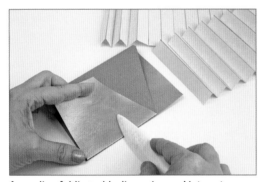

Accordion folding adds dimension and interest, whether making smaller, carefully ruled, uniform folds or larger asymmetrical folds. For best results, use a bone folder to crease and smooth your paper.

These tri-fold accordion cards provide ample space for words and design elements.

ACETATE

A clear or frosted vinyl sheet used to cover the top of card fronts. The acetate may include designs and words. Be sure to select the correct acetate for inkjet or laser printers.

Print the image directly onto acetate. Then place it over a painted—or as shown here, gilded—background.

Place a botanical image printed on acetate onto card stock with a square, die-cut aperture. When opened, the card resembles a stained glass window.

AGING AND DISTRESSING

Techniques that give objects or papers a vintage or antique effect, including ready-made patterned papers, cardstock, photos, embellishments, or found objects. *See also* Shabby Chic and Wrinkling.

Color Aging—Use colored chalks, colored pencils, ink pens, and food items, such as coffee grounds, tea, vegetables, or juices, to color torn edges or highlight a particular word or quote.

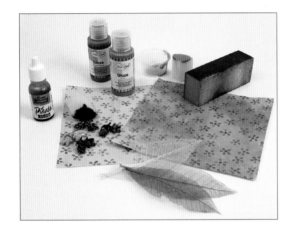

HOW-TO BASICS: **COLOR AGING**

1. Soak, sponge, or use cotton swabs or tissues to wet the paper.
2. Start with a light touch and apply more if needed.
3. Lightly sponge, spritz, or brush earth-tone-colored inks, whitewash glazes, or chalks onto pre-printed and hand-stamped paper, leaves, and hardware to provide cards with a vintage or nostalgic feeling.

Air-Dry Clay

A group of clays that dry without the addition of heat. Always check the manufacturer's packaging to be sure that the clay is acid-free and suitable for paper crafts. Air-dry clays are more brittle and fragile than other varieties of clay. *See also* Clay.

An air-dry clay tablet mounted on a card makes an ordinary card extraordinary.

Album

A blank book used to store photographs, greeting cards, and memorabilia. *See also* Card Album.

Altered Art

In this contemporary art form, recycled objects originally intended for practical purposes, such as books, advertising, and photographs, are turned into works of art by any creative means.

Andachtsbilder

A German New Year's greeting from the 15th century, commonly made from copper plates as well as hand-colored woodcuts. Andachtsbilder are not greeting cards in the traditional sense, but pictures with Christian themes that were shared as gifts.

Angel Company

A term identifying any company that allows a consumer to use its rubberstamp or paper images to create one-of-a-kind products for resale. Policies vary widely, so you'll need to contact each manufacturer about copyright policies.

ANNIVERSARY CARD

A card sent to commemorate a past wedding, either your own or someone else's. These cards tend to emphasize the love or bond between two people. Here are some samples to inspire you. *See also* Special Occasion Card.

ANTI-STATIC PAD

A small bag filled with a static-inhibiting powder. Rubbing a paper surface with the pad reduces static electricity, keeping stray embossing-powder granules from being accidentally heated. It is also used by calligraphers to prevent inks from bleeding into the paper due to static electricity. Anti-static pads are used to reduce static electricity from the acetate windows in shaker boxes.

APERTURE

A die-cut opening or window of any shape in a card.

Whether using the cardstock itself, overlays or even mica tile, an aperture usually frames the focal point or the greeting.

Appliqué

French for *applied*. In paper crafts, any detailed ornament that is adhered to a paper surface rather than cut from the paper itself is considered an appliqué.

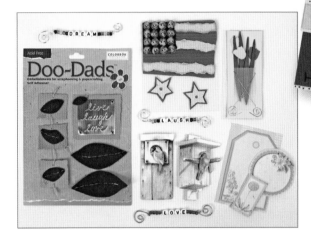

One large designer appliqué is proportionately just right for this card. Handwritten words and dotted outlines add further design interest.

Manufacturers are ingenious about matching dies with designs, showing card makers how to make appliqués using simple layering techniques.

Charming handmade appliqué letters whimsically explode from a flower-festooned tin mailbox. You can purchase appliqués ready-made or make them yourself!

Combine ribbons, buttons, and paper flowers to produce your own appliqué designs. Net ribbon provides a high-end, shabby-chic appeal.

ARCHIVAL

A non-technical term indicating that a material is permanent, durable, or chemically stable. Also a material that can be used safely for preservation purposes, although there are no quantifiable standards that describe how long an archival material will last.

ARTIST TRADING CARD

A contemporary art form derived from sports-themed trading cards. The standard dimension for an authentic ATC is 2½ x 3½ inches. The card becomes a small piece of art that can be traded or given as a gift, but never sold.

Whether elegantly made for business using gild and a mica overlay, or collaged and painted as a greeting card insert, artist trading cards are fun to give and even more fun to trade.

ASSEMBLAGE

A term describing objects collected and assembled to create a harmonious work of art. Generally, the components are three-dimensional, not made by the artist, and not originally intended as an art material.

An imaginative arrangement of buttons, fabric, ribbon, rhinestones, and rick-rack creates a charming and colorful assemblage.

Artfully combined, fanciful elements are assembled and hand-sewn into a plastic, tree-shaped pouch. The background, while colorful, is carefully composed to accentuate the tree shape

ATG

An economical, pressure-sensitive dry adhesive, ATG can be applied by hand or mechanically dispensed and is evenly distributed from a liner-paper.

The assemblage cards shown here are assembled using ATG. ATG prevents paper from cockling or buckling and provides easy multiple repositioning and smooth layering. *See also* Adhesive.

A bit of wire, an electric staple,
and a mica ring become a geometric assembly
with a decidedly masculine appearance.

Paste-paper backgrounds, jewelry parts, and funky gilded telephone buttons
are positively inspirational when artfully combined.

BACKGROUND PAPER

Almost any patterned, neutral-colored, or handmade paper used to emphasize a focal point or tie together a complex composition.

A colorful sampling of background papers. Just think of the possibilities!

BACK-PRINT

An impression that occurs when the edges of a rubber polymer die or foam stamp are inadvertently stamped onto the paper. To avoid this, either don't rock the stamp or trim excess edges with a craft knife. *See also* Stamping.

BALANCE

An aesthetically pleasing integration of visual elements. Balance is determined by the size, shape, and visual weight of the parts of a composition. *See also* Composition.

The Encyclopedia of Greeting Card Tools & Techniques

BARGELLO

A style borrowed from needlework techniques in which paper strips are adhered in horizontal sets, then cut and arranged in vertical steps to produce interesting geometric designs that often have an undulating look.

HOW-TO BASICS: **BARGELLO**

1. Select complementary papers that suit the occasion, and cut them into varying widths.

2. Lay the strips on an adhesive sheet or tape them from behind so the long edges touch.

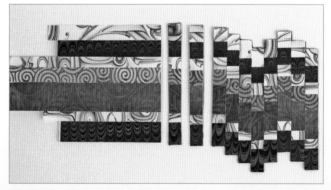

3. Cut the strips vertically. Stagger the strips, taping them together on the back to form a pattern.

4. Mount the completed piece onto the card.

BATIK

A method of dyeing borrowed from an Indonesian textile technique in which a pattern is drawn with wax on paper. The paper is dipped into inks, dyes, or watercolors, and the wax prevents the color from penetrating the pattern areas. You can obtain multicolored and blended effects by scraping off the initial wax pattern and repeating the dyeing process several times.

HOW-TO BASICS: BATIK

1. Select a light-colored paper. (Papers with cotton fibers work best.)

2. Cover your work area with newspaper.

3. Draw a design using an unlit candle, a crayon, or paraffin wax. Each provides a different effect.

4. Crumple the paper into a ball once you've drawn the design.

5. Smooth out the paper, and dip it in a shallow pan filled with a light-colored ink or dye. Wait for the paper to completely absorb the color.

6. Allow the paper to dry thoroughly.

7. If desired, add wax patterns over the inked areas. Dip the paper into the ink again, this time using a darker shade.

8. Allow the paper to dry.

9. Remove the wax by scraping it off with a credit card or by ironing the paper between sheets of newspaper.

You can create distinctive-looking cards with batik, a technique more commonly used with clothing, fabrics, and pillows. Small batiks make charming framable cards.

BEAD

A small decorative object pierced for threading or stringing made from glass, polymer, wood, plastic, or other material. *See also* Microbead.

may the Light of This season shine upon you all through the year

Beads add appeal—and depth—to greeting cards. With the endless variety readily available, you will never run out of ideas for beaded cards.

BLEACH

A technique using household bleach to discolor or alter card stock by removing color from the paper.

CAUTION—Bleach is very strong-smelling. If you are sensitive to chemicals, ventilate your work area well or work outdoors. Read all safety warnings on the container before use. Also make sure your work surface is protected. This technique is suitable for adults only.

TIP

Creating card designs with bleach is fun and innovative. Every paper will perform differently, and some barely work at all. Experimentation is important.

HOW-TO BASICS: BLEACH STAMPING

1. Place a pad of paper towels in a small plastic pan.
2. Pour in enough bleach to dampen the paper towels.
3. Tap your stamp onto the bleach-soaked paper towels.
4. Stamp your paper. It may take several minutes for the bleach to finish processing.
5. Use a heat tool to speed up the process.
6. Wash your stamp in warm, soapy water.

HOW-TO BASICS: BLEACH STENCILING

1. Place a pad of paper towels in a small plastic pan.
2. Pour in enough bleach to dampen the paper towels.
3. Use masking tape to fix a stencil firmly to your paper.
4. Dampen a stencil brush or sponge by tapping it in the bleach.
5. Tap the brush gently through the stencil.
6. Carefully lift off the stencil, and wash it in clear water. It may take several minutes for the bleach to finish processing.
7. Use a heat tool to speed up the process.

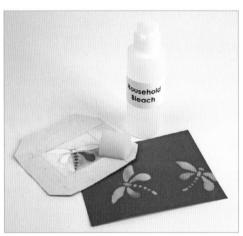

Bleach stenciling supplies

Bleach stamping supplies

BLEED

The migration of ink, paint, or adhesive through or across paper. This process may occur immediately upon application or over time. *Bleed* is also a printer's term used to refer to color (ink, paint, or paper) that runs all the way to the edge of a trimmed page.

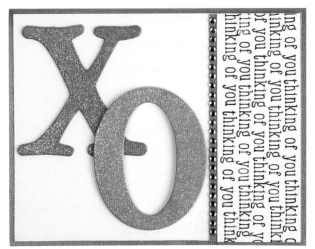

Running color or words right off the edge of a card creates a unique design element. "Bleeding off" can anchor, border, or frame the main design.

::: HOW-TO BASICS: **BLEACH WATERBRUSHING** :::

1. Fill a waterbrush with a mixture of five parts water and one part bleach. Mark the waterbrush, so you use it only for bleach.

2. Paint or draw on colored card stock as you would with a watercolor brush.

3. Use the waterbrush to remove watercolor or ink from any areas you'd like to highlight.

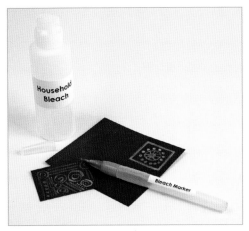

Bleach waterbrushing supplies

BLENDER PEN

A writing utensil filled with a clear fluid formulated to work with solvent-based or water-based markers, watercolors, chalks, or inks. By stroking from the outside in, the fluid pushes a layer of color, causing it to become a lighter shade of the same color. Or, it may mingle with two colors to create a third.

BLIND EMBOSSING

A technique in which a raised image is created on paper under pressure by an engraved metal plate. *See also* Emboss.

Simple mechanical devices are now available with interchangeable stencils giving card makers another alternative to dry emboss. Operating like a punch, they provide just the right pressure to lightweight card stock to produce a small, but perfect image every time.

BLITZER

A hand tool used with standard brush-type markers. Its squeezable bulb releases air over the point of a marker, which creates an airbrush effect.

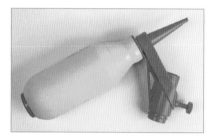

BLOCKING

See Color Blocking.

BONE FOLDER

A smooth hand tool made of bone or plastic used for folding, scoring, and creasing papers or for pressing out air bubbles and wrinkles when gluing papers and fabrics to other surfaces.

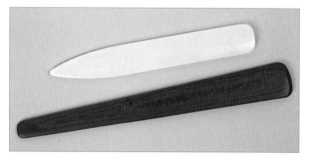

BORDER

A decorative edge, title, line, or design used to surround a page. Borders may be self-adhesive stickers, die-cuts, templates, punch-out die cuts, or photos themselves.

Die-cuts and punch-out die cuts add dimension to a card. The possibilities are endless!

Borders come in every conceivable style, material, color, and design. This laser-cut lace border works with all kinds of Victorian, floral, or kitschy designs.

Whimsical, patterned sticker borders even work as a frame. This card actually has multiple layers: a glitter shaker box, coral, a border, and fish and turtle appliqués.

BOTTLE CAP

Easy to find or purchase, bottle caps can be flattened, decorated, and used on frames for photographs, letters, or words. Consider aging, painting, or adding glitter to them to coordinate with any card.

Smashed with a hammer or run over by car tires, bottle caps have long been used as dimensional elements. Here, one is stuffed, along with pretty beads, into a wire mesh tube.

Several bottle caps are evenly smashed and enhanced with die-cuts made with a universal paper crafter's tool.

BOX

A container for storing keepsake cards, available in a myriad of styles. For a bedroom, consider a hatbox or shoebox wallpapered to match the room. For the living room, choose a more formal photograph box or small wooden trunk. *See also* Organization.

BOXED CARD SET

A set of greeting cards often consisting of one particular style, theme, or design created by a single artist.

A small scarf box decorated with a medallion is ideal for a group of medallion cards, each sporting a flower or star. A perfect gift for family, friends, and the elderly, this boxed set needs only a pretty pen and a book of stamps to make it a very special present.

Dragonflies, each different in style, provide a common theme for a boxed set of cards. Even the box top is stamped.

BRAYER

A small hand tool resembling a paint roller used in paper crafts to make background papers or to apply pressure to layers of paper. The most common brayers are made of rubber, hard foam, acrylic, or sponge.

HOW-TO BASICS: **BRAYERING**

1. Brayers come in many different sizes.

2. Roll a brayer several times over a multicolored ink pad.

3. After unloading the ink onto the background paper, overstamp and emboss one or several designs in white, or add a photo. Bleaching techniques and stickers also work nicely on these backgrounds.

Thinking of you

When brayering with ink, it is especially nice to use a bleached stamping technique, creating a unique focal point.

Add small cut-out shapes to a brayered surface to provide contrast and texture to a card. This card also has a stamped and embossed greeting.

BRISTOL BOARD

A stiff, heavy paper whose caliper ranges upward from 0.006 inches.

BRUSH MARKER

A water-based marking pen with a long, broad tip. *See also* Markers.

BURNISH

To rub with a tool that causes an especially smooth or polished surface. In paper crafts, a bone folder is most often used for smoothing and burnishing. *See also* Bone Folder.

BUTTON

A fastener made of plastic, metal, or bone often used as an embellishment in card making to add texture or color, or to define corners.

Button cards

CALIPER

The average thickness of a single sheet paper as determined by measuring the thickness of different sheets and averaging the results.

CALLIGRAPHY

The art of decorative handwriting. A calligrapher's principal tools are a pen, various nibs or pen points, a brush, felt-tip markers, ballpoint pens, and usually water-based ink. Calligraphy requires patience and attention to detail, which are more important than artistic flair.

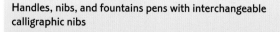

Handles, nibs, and fountains pens with interchangeable calligraphic nibs

Card Album

A scrapbook for storing keepsake cards. Mount cards into a pretty, room-coordinated album where family and friends can view them easily.

HOW-TO BASICS:
COFFEE TABLE CARD ALBUM

1. Organize cards by the month and year received, by event, or occasion. Consider making an album for each member of the family.

2. Cut the card and display the front and the inside side-by-side. If a message is personal, tape the card closed.

3. Write the artist, date, and event under each card with a pen or marker.

4. Mount a photo of the sender, if available, next to the card.

Card Making

The art of creating a special message of greeting or other sentiment from a folded piece of card stock. Cards are usually given on special occasions, such as birthdays, Christmas, Valentine's Day or other holidays. Hallmark Cards is the largest mass-producer of greeting cards in the U.S. *See also* Card Submission.

Card Stock

Sturdy paper available in a variety of weights, colors, and textures. Card stock is used for paper crafts. Generally about the thickness of an index card, card stock comes in matte, gloss, satin, foil, and metallic finishes. *See also* Paper and Ready-Made Card Stock.

Liz Sewald,
Card Making

"There's nothing quite like the 'I made that' feeling when looking at a card you've just completed," says Liz Sewald. "I believe anyone can make a card and experience that feeling of success. I've seen so many beautiful cards in my travels … and so many of them are worthy of framing!"

As a designer of art-card samples using materials from the dozens of art, craft,

and scrapbooking manufacturers she represents, Liz admits she got to this place in a roundabout way. "I began as a printmaker and mixed-media artist, but settled on making art cards 11 years ago because it offered an instant gratifica-

tion," says the mother of two children.

Along the way, Liz found that her love of card making could be shared with others through teaching and product education. "Just play," she says. "With the sheer abundance of materials available to card makers, you could use a different product or technique every day for a year, and you'd barely scratch the surface of what's really available."

She's quick to point out, "Crayons and typing paper work, too. After all, with card giving, it's really the thought that counts."

CHALK

Geologically speaking, the chalk used by crafters is actually gypsum, not natural chalk. A sedimentary rock substance, the art material called chalk is ground, pigmented, and then formed and held into shapes using light binders. Chalk is an alkaline substance, versatile and useful for a wide range of paper craft projects and techniques, including shading, highlighting, distressing, and coloring paper.

Chalk comes in a large variety of sizes, shapes, and colors.

Cards made with chalk techniques

HOW-TO BASICS: **CHALKING**

While chalking works on most papers with tooth, embossed papers really showcase the product, highlighting the raised areas with color. Here, blending several analogous colors using a soft applicator, gives the background paper a "watercolory" appearance—a perfect choice for this marker/blender pen focal image.

The Encyclopedia of Greeting Card Tools & Techniques

CHALKBOARD SPRAY PAINT

PRODUCT TIP

Spray several sheets of card stock with chalkboard spray paint. Have it ready for those creative days. Always use spray paints outdoors with plenty of cross ventilation.

CHALKING TOOL

An implement for applying chalk to paper. May include sponges or sponge daubers, cotton swabs, or sponge cosmetics applicators.

CHALKING TIPS

- To prevent smearing, place a piece of computer paper over the majority of the artwork and rest your hand on that, lifting and moving it as necessary.

- A centuries-old artist's tool, the maulstick is a long stick with a cushion on one end that rests on the table surface. It is used to steady the working hand, while keeping it above the artwork. A quick and easy substitute for a maulstick is a ruler.

- It may be necessary to spray a fixative on a finished chalking to prevent smearing.

CHANUKAH CARD

Here are a couple of samples to show you just how creative Chanukah cards can be.

Happy Chanukah!

CHROMOLITHOGRAPHY

Any lithograph printed in at least three colors. The process was developed in the early 1800s by German printer Alois Senefelder and the term coined in 1837 by Frenchman Godefroy Engelmann. Widely used in the production of Victorian greeting cards, chromolithography produced millions of inexpensive multi-color images, providing affordable greeting cards to the masses.

CLAY

Any malleable material able to be molded and fashioned into a dimensional motif. This broad definition includes many types of clay. *See also* Air-Dry Clay and Polymer Clay.

CLEAR ART STAMP

A tool made from a film negative and hardened liquid polymer, clear stamps provide artists a transparent view for correct image placement. An alternative to the traditional rubber stamp, polymer stamps may yellow or harden over time, especially if exposed to sunlight, indoor lighting, oil-based products, solvent inks, acetone, or bleach. *See also* Stamping.

CLIP ART

Ready-made pieces of printed or computerized art. Clip Art can be copied, scanned, or printed from the computer directly onto card stock or paper. It is usually copyright-free, or may have a fee for limited use.

Clip art comes in paper and electronic forms. Use whichever best fits your needs.

Susan Pickering Rothamel,
Collage Artist

A self-proclaimed pack rat, paper aficio-
nado, and collector of exotic stuff, Susan
Pickering Rothamel says, "It's only natural
that as a career, I've explored collage and
mixed media as my primary form of
'arting.'"

But, when all is said and done, card making
is where all the leftover bits come together
and satisfy the urge to create—instantly! It
is not only great fun, Susan claims, but it's
fairly quick to take those leftover "art
starts"—the paper-scraps of this and
that—add a few fibers or fabric, and then
adhere them all to a piece of card, or alter a
ready-made greeting card.

Designing your own personal cards is
immensely satisfying. It may take a little
more time, but the joy of hearing a family
member or neighbor say, "We always look
forward to seeing what you made this year"
makes it worth the investment.

"So," says Susan, "I'll round out Friday and
Saturday to plan my cards—deciding on
the design for this year's Christmas
offerings. On Sunday, I shall ask my brain
to rest."

Susan is president of USArtQuest.
www.usartquest.com

The diversity of patterns and colors
available in papers today can make
anyone's brain go into overdrive. "I
marvel at how many things can be made
of, covered with, or otherwise embellished with paper. On Monday I can
paper-texture a wall, and Tuesday collage
a countertop. On Wednesday I can make
unique art for the local gallery, and on
Thursday fashion my own bathroom
accessories. Paper is divinely versatile,
becoming whatever you want it to be."

COLOR

A visual experience that can be described as having quantifiable dimensions of hue, saturation, and brightness or lightness. As an element of design, color draws attention, evokes emotions, and conveys messages.

Colors on a card can come from many sources: the paper, the ink, embellishments, and more.

COLOR THEORY TERMS

Analogous Color—Colors adjacent to each other on the color wheel. One color is used as a dominant color, while others are used to enhance the imagery.

Secondary Color—A color formed by mixing equal parts of two primary colors. In art, secondary colors are orange, green, and purple.

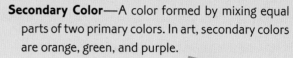

Primary Color—Any of three colors from which all others can be made by mixing. In art, primary colors are red, yellow, and blue.

Tertiary Color—A color formed by mixing equal parts of a primary color and a secondary color. Also known as intermediate color.

Complementary Color—A color directly opposite another on the color wheel. Also known as color harmonies, complementary colors contrast the most and create visual excitement when placed side by side. When complements of equal and correct proportions are mixed, they will always form a gray tone.

Contrast—The degree of difference between light and dark areas in an image. High contrast has little or no intermediate tones; medium contrast implies a good spread from shadows and some middle tones; and low contrast implies a small spread of color.

Monochromatic—A color scheme that uses one (or "mono") color (or "chroma") in different shades.

COLOR THEORY TERMS

Pastel Color—The mixture of any primary, secondary, or tertiary color with white to achieve a less saturated color.

Temperature—A numerical description of the color of light as measured in Kelvin degrees.

Warm Color—Hues that by association suggest warmth, such as red, orange, and yellow.

Cool Color—Hues that by association give an impression of coolness, such as blue and green.

COLOR BLOCKING

A technique in which geometric areas or blocks of two or more colors form a design element, background, or focal point.

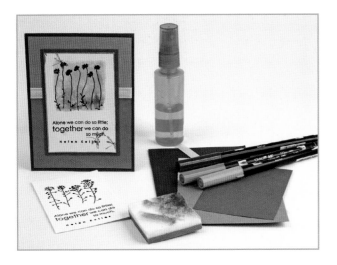

Using a cut square sponge, color the square with several watercolor markers, then spritz with water. Stamp the sponge onto a stamped and embossed image or foil sticker. Successive stampings produce lighter color blocks.

COLORFAST

An object or paint that resists the harmful UV rays of light, acid, and heat. Also called lightfast.

COLOR WASH

A technique in which diluted watercolors are brushed on over permanent images or colored paper for a background. Avoid muddy washes by using analogous color schemes. *See also* Watercolor.

Some examples of color washed cards and paper to show you its possibilities. Use your imagination, and you'll never run out of ideas.

COLOR WHEEL

A circular diagram in which colors are arranged sequentially so that related colors are next to each other and complementary colors are opposite.

COLORED PENCIL

A drawing or writing tool made using a dye or pigment in a wax base material, instead of the graphite of a traditional pencil. The quality of the wax determines how consistently and smoothly the colors blend when sketching, drawing, or shading.

Good quality colored pencils are so versatile, you'll want to have them on hand whenever you make cards.

TIP

The white of the fish eye is shaped using a darker color on the bottom, suggesting a shadow, and then faded up. Add a complementary color (red) to the greens in order to attract attention. The black dot in the center was added to create the iris, with a white highlight added for effect.

To make the card above, you begin by applying bleach to selective areas of a fish stamp and stamp the paper. Notice that the body of the fish has been bleached, but not the fin areas. When it's dry, clean the stamp and ink it with permanent black ink. Stamp the fish impression over the bleached area. Highlight the eye and other select areas with colored pencils, and use bright cardstock to frame and emphasize the colored penciled accents.

COMPLEMENTARY COLOR

See Color.

COMPOSITION

The way the creative elements, colors, and shapes are organized into a whole that is satisfying to the viewer. Creative variables such as balance, color, and texture are all subjective considerations, that when combined form an image that is pleasing to the eye. The main element of composition is balance and the shape of the unused space, as well as element proportion. Composition may be symmetrical, off-center, or asymmetrically balanced.

- Compositional balance is determined by the visual weight of each element. Weight can be calculated by the size of the object, the value (dark objects weigh more than light objects), and the texture.

- When the contrast between elements is too great, balance is lost.

- Proportion and size should also be considered when checking for balance.

- Balance may be symmetrical or asymmetrical. Symmetrical design often creates a static card—focusing the eye in one area—but also produces a strong focal point. Asymmetrical design requires a skillful arrangement of elements with different visual weights, which can create a visually dynamic card.

COMPOSITION GUIDELINES

While composition rules are meant to be broken, here are a few guidelines to create more visually pleasing designs:

- Use the "Rule of Thirds." Divide a design into thirds both vertically and horizontally. Where those lines meet is a good place to put the focal point(s) of a layout.

- Use the same element in odd numbers one, three, or five times on the same page.

- Create contrast in your pages through use of color, size, or texture of the elements.

Well-balanced cards

COMPUTER CARD

A method of making cards using scanned, digital, and computer-generated imagery and words. Computer cards come in as many forms as your computer can generate. Printing old photos in sepia, using clip art programs, or making your own greeting (such as "baby shower") and adding some personalized handmade artwork are just a few of the options available to card makers.

Pam-lam

I wanted to get you something nice at Pomeroys

for your birthday—but I couldn't find a single thing...

a baby shower

CONDOLENCE CARD

When you want to express your sympathies, nothing quite touches the heart like a handmade card. Here are a few samples to show you how.

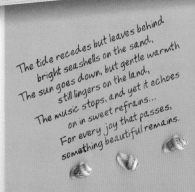

Sympathy

Designed here to express sympathy, this tulip card could actually be adapted for nearly any occasion. Keep handy a variety of sticker greetings such as Sympathy, Happy Birthday, Get Well, or Happy Anniversary. Make the cards in advance, and personalize them as needed.

When someone you *love* becomes a *memory* the memory becomes a *Treasure*

The tide recedes but leaves behind
bright seashells on the sand,
The sun goes down, but gentle warmth
still lingers on the land,
The music stops, and yet it echoes
on in sweet refrains...
For every joy that passes,
something beautiful remains.

CONFETTI

Small pieces of colored plastic or paper made to be thrown during a celebratory event. In cardmaking, it may be added to envelopes for a cheerful opening, or glued to a card surface.

CONTRAST

See Color.

COOL COLOR

See Color.

COPYRIGHT

A legal notice that protects "original works of authorship" both published and unpublished, that are expressed in a tangible form, but not the ideas themselves. The symbol for a copyrighted material is ©.

Die-cut letters, all glittery in red, are ideal for this holiday. The confetti adds to the festive nature of the card. Notice, too, how the holly berries repeat the square confetti pattern.

While often just sprinkled into the envelope, confetti is also a great card embellishment. Strategically placed and adhered directly to a fabric flower, it adds a cheerful celebratory touch, without the mess that loose confetti can make.

C

CORNER EDGER

Scissors and other devices that cut paper while creating specialty corners or decorative patterns.

Corner edgers can help you frame your focal point with style.

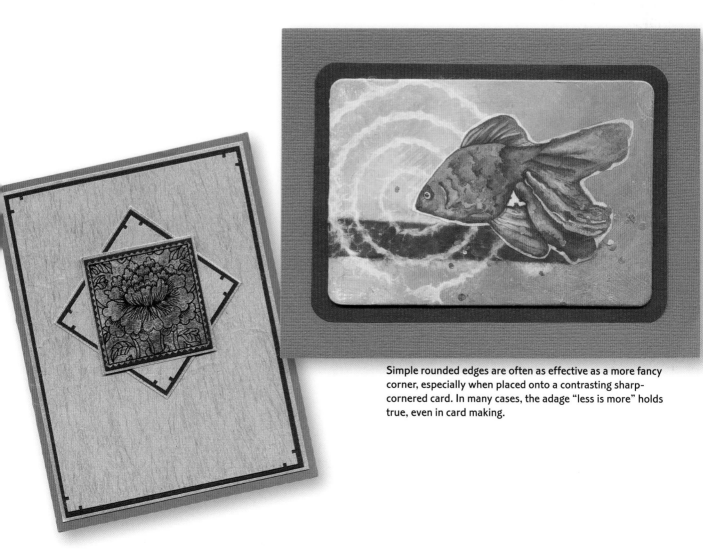

Simple rounded edges are often as effective as a more fancy corner, especially when placed onto a contrasting sharp-cornered card. In many cases, the adage "less is more" holds true, even in card making.

Corner Punch

A device used to pierce a photograph or paper corner for decorative purposes. *See also* Punch.

Corner Rounder

A punch or scissors used for rounding the corners of photographs and paper. *See also* Corner Edger and Punch.

Corrugated Paper

A heavy paper made to resemble even rows of valleys and mountains. Corrugated papers provide texture and dimension, as well as an opportunity to fill in and embellish the valleys. *See also* Paper.

Add a corrugated section as a way to further embellish a card, using a fine tip adhesive applicator in the paper valleys and some gorgeous microbeads.

CORRUGATOR

A hand tool that ripples paper. Also known as a crimper.

With tools like these, you can create new looks and special effects even with regular paper!

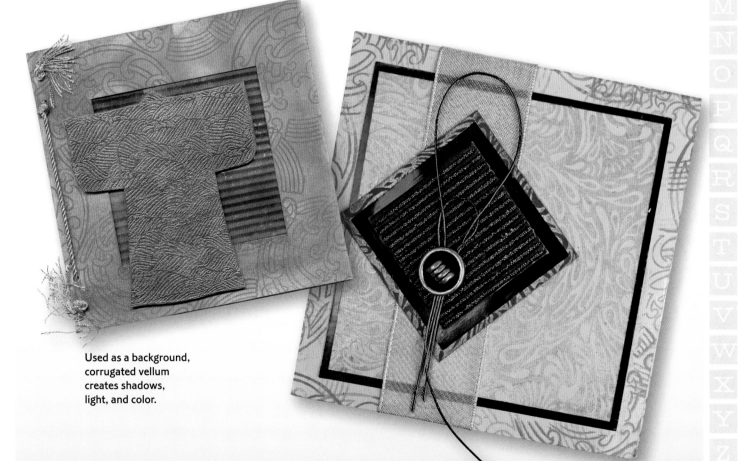

Used as a background, corrugated vellum creates shadows, light, and color.

Corrugated paper adds textural interest to any card, but with the valleys filled with micro-beads, it becomes a much stronger image.

A technique in which a wax-based crayon and water-based media repel one another. Depending on the paper or crayon used, the repelling of the paint allows the color of the crayon to be highlighted, or to become a highlight.

Used as a resist, crayons produce mixed, but surprising and interesting results. Simply draw or trace a design. Wash over it with watercolors. Use different papers to produce different results. Here glossy card stock actually resists some of the watercolor too.

HOW-TO BASICS:
CRAYON RESIST – VARIATION 1

1. Draw a design or picture with crayons. Light colors work the best.
2. Press hard with the crayons so they will show up under the paint.
3. When complete, lightly brush dark paint over the picture.
4. The areas of crayon will resist the dark paint.

HOW-TO BASICS:
CRAYON RESIST – VARIATION 2

1. Using a glossy card stock, stamp an image in black or other dark ink.
2. Color an area to highlight with a white crayon.
3. Sponge inks to cover the entire card.
4. Use a paper towel to remove ink from the crayoned area.

OTHER CRAYON RESIST THEMES

- Antique metallic crayoning, using black or dark tempera paints.
- Crackle finish the paper by crumpling a completely crayoned paper, then cover with paint.
- Try various colors to produce different effects.
- For rainbow effects, cover the entire surface of the paper with various colors, and then apply a thick water-based paint. When it's dry, scrape off the paint in specific areas.

CRIMPER

A tool used to corrugate paper or card stock. *See also* Corrugator.

CROP

To trim the edges of an image, often to improve its composition.

This faux lace background paper made using ATG and mica flakes appears more finished, as well as balanced, when cropped and framed with a narrow frame of colored card stock.

CROP MARK

A line or mark indicating where the pages or photographs will be trimmed.

CUTTING MAT

See Self-Healing Cutting Mat.

CYANOACRYLATE

An extremely fast-cure adhesive available in various thicknesses and cure times. Cyanoacrylate adhesives may yellow or become brittle over time and should have limited use, adhering only the most difficult nonporous surfaces and polymer clay. *See also* Adhesives.

D

DEBOSSING

A technique in which paper areas recess, or go down, rather than rise up. *See also* Emboss.

DECKLE EDGE

A deckle edge can be defined as:

1. The naturally rough or feathered edge of untrimmed handmade paper. 2. A type of feathered edge imitated in commercial papers. 3. Hand-cut paper edges created using special scissors, cutters, or rulers to resemble untrimmed handmade papers.

HOW-TO BASICS: **DECKLED FOCAL POINT**

1. Deckling is not just used for paper edges, but also for the focal point itself. Select a soft fibered paper, and use a pre-formed hard shape as a template.

2. Follow along the edge with a water-loaded brush.

3. Gently tear along the wet area using your fingers.

4. When dry, mount the deckle-edged heart shape onto crisp, cut card stock.

HOW-TO BASICS: **DECKLE RULER**

Tearing along a special deckle-edge ruler lets you create a funky border for almost any type of paper.

HOW-TO BASICS:
WET & TEAR DECKLING

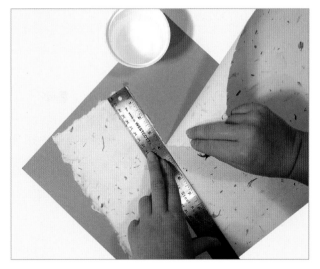

1. To create a deckle edge without using deckle-edge scissors, place a ruler along the line to be deckled and run a wet paintbrush along the edge.

2. When the paper turns dark and wet, slowly and evenly tear the paper up and against the ruler's edge. A soft deckling will occur.

DECORATIVE ITEM

Any creative element, such as specialty papers, die cuts, stickers, eyelets, buttons, or other materials used in card making.

DECORATIVE SCISSORS

A hand tool used to cut paper, fabric, or card stock with one or many decorative pattern styles on the blade.

You can find decorative scissors in craft stores. Some even come in multi-unit packages that give you a wide array of choices whenever you need a deckle edge.

DECOUPAGE

A decorative paper art technique using carefully cut figurative paper illustrations. The cut pieces are then pasted onto nearly any surface. The technique was made popular in Victorian times, when young women would decoupage everything from floor screens to furniture, and boxes to album covers.

As long as it is figurative, nearly any type of paper can be used to create decoupage cards. Gift wrap loaded with colorful geckos provide plenty of images to cut, piece, and paste. Whether crawling across the card, lined up in rows, or a single image as a focal point, decoupage offers tremendous design opportunities.

DEGRADATION

Any product that is initially low in acid but becomes increasingly more acidic over time due to chemical reactions from aging or migration. Examples of degradation: paper yellowing or becoming brittle, or tape becoming yellow or losing its stickiness.

DELTIOLOGY

The hobby of collecting postcards.

DIE

Cut metal motifs, shapes, or letters, usually embedded into wood and rubber forms, used for cutting paper into the shape of the metal design. Also an engraved stamp used for impressing an image or design.

Whether a single branch of holly or a delicately cut Japanese paper, creative card making is just a snip away. The card entitled "Dream" is both decoupaged and paper-enameled.

DIE CUTTING

A method of using sharp steel-ruled dies and pressure rollers to cut various shapes, generally called die cuts.

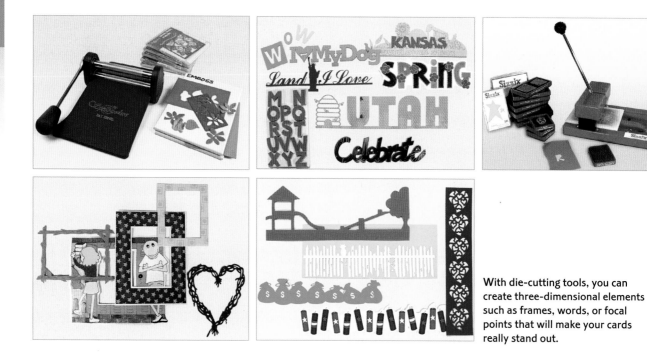

With die-cutting tools, you can create three-dimensional elements such as frames, words, or focal points that will make your cards really stand out.

TIPS

Because there are dozens of die-cut systems on the market, select one that fits the budget and has a universal component to its design. These offer the most options as your card making skills evolve.

Use an emery board to smooth the edges of a die cut, gently stroking the edge in one direction.

Begin with the direct-to-paper technique on glossy card stock and then die cut the flowers. Layer each flower individually with their separately cut centers, and then slightly bend the petals to give them dimension.

Not just die cut, these fish have also been embossed. The embossing is highlighted with ink. Beautiful Asian papers and embellishments accentuate the authentic chopsticks, which are being given as the gift itself.

This charming tri-fold card displays fanciful embossed flowers, colorfully chalked and scattered onto bright pink borders.

DIGITAL IMAGE

An image obtained by electronic data and storage rather than by the chemical processes in traditional photography. Obtained by using digital cameras, camcorders, scanners, or other devices, digital imagery captures and stores pictures without film. When printed, the images are considered color photographs.

DIMENSIONAL ADHESIVE

A PVA or acrylic-based adhesive that dries to raised, clear glass-like or a raised opaque finish. These adhesives are used for special effects and for their specialty adhering qualities. *See also* Adhesive.

Card with digital image

DIMENSIONAL EMBOSSING

The use of stencils and relief products, such as clay, artist cements, and pastes, to bring added depth to a raised or lowered image or word(s). Also known as Relief Embossing and Dimensional Stenciling. *See also* Emboss.

1. Spread the cement evenly and in one swipe, if possible, through a plastic or brass stencil.

2. Immediately clean the stencil with water. While the cement is still wet, sprinkle on bits of mica, glitter, or other small particles. When the design is completely covered, allow it to dry thoroughly.

Begin by color blocking with inks, and then apply the dimensionally stenciled design. When it's complete, color the design with pearlescent paint.

After stenciling the design and allowing it to dry thoroughly, use various inks on the surface to create the stained glass effect.

Use several different stencils to create a sampler piece. When the cement is dry, gild the entire area, bringing a continuity and sophistication of design.

85

DIRECT TO PAPER

A technique of moving ink or paint from one place to another, either by using the inkpad or other sponge-like device, directly onto card stock.

Stamp the same image onto small scraps of paper and cut them out. Stamp and emboss the images onto card stock. Use the scraps as a mask, fitting them over the card stock images and begin using ink pads to smooth ink color over the background. When the scrap is removed, the stamped areas can be colored in separately, using markers, ink, chalks, or sparkling watercolors.

DISTRESSED PAPER

A piece of paper that has been transformed into an older-looking version of itself by wrinkling, folding, wetting, sanding, or otherwise damaging the sheet.

DOMINO

A game piece, altered and used as a card embellishment or focal point.

Collage a pattern directly onto a domino and mount it as the focal point on a color-blocked greeting card.

DOUBLE MOUNT

An art or photo framing technique using two papers, each progressively larger than the original focal point.

The colors and textures of the handmade paper feature pretty deckle edging. The leaf imagery is stronger after double-mounting than it would be mounted directly to the card made from a plain brown paper bag.

E-CARD

A greeting card chosen and sent via the Internet. E-cards may be traditional in style or personalized, and they may include music and moving components (animation).

EASTER CARD

Although it's not generally a holiday many people associate with card-giving, Easter can inspire you to produce very creative cards. There are two sides to Easter: the religious and the juvenile. Here are some samples that reflect both. *See also* Holiday Celebration Card.

Happy Easter

With Love

Believe

ELEMENT

As the word pertains to paper crafting: any photograph, embellishment, color, paper layer, or design shape used within a card's composition.

EMBELLISHMENT

Any slightly or fully dimensional decorative element that enhances a card.

A simply stamped butterfly becomes dazzling when rhinestones are added. Add even more sparkle using double-sided tape and Mica D'Lights.

Beads, buttons, cabochons, words, and other objects can all become embellishments on a greeting card. Don't be shy—experiment!

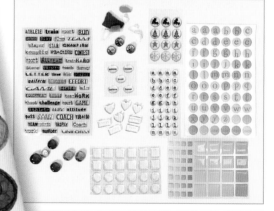

Grace Taormina,
Embellishments

Grace Taormina's love for creating has led her on an interesting and varied career path. She has designed and imported women's apparel, worked in sales and marketing in the gift industry, and labored as a teacher and product designer in the art and craft industry, serving as the "go-to" designer for Rubber Stampede and Delta Creative.

Grace has explored the creative potential of rubber-stamp art in her books *The Complete Guide to Rubber Stamping* and *The Complete Guide to Decorative Stamping*, as well as in many popular magazines and in guest appearances on the *Carol Duvall Show* and *Decorating with Style*.

She lives near San Francisco and says, "Even with all I have done, I most enjoy teaching others the joy of embellishing their art and life with creativity."

Shadow stamping provides a colorful background to the silhouette stamped image. Use a ribbon to enhance the one-third composition rule. The dragonfly is not only an appropriate embellishment for the subject matter, but it also draws the eye into the composition and ties the layers together.

EMBOSS

To create a raised or lowered image or word by using one of several methods, including pressure, heat, or resins. *See also* Blind Embossing, Dimensional Embossing, Dry Embossing, and Heat Embossing.

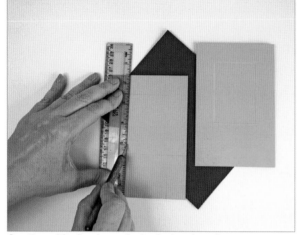

Creating a blind embossed raised edge gives the appearance of another paper layer, or even a frame for the artwork or focal point.

EMBOSSED PAPER

Paper that has been machine- or hand-embossed.

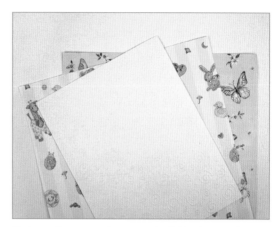

Embossed paper makes a wonderful background—as well as producing exceptional highlights—for your greeting cards.

Embossed paper looks spectacular when aged with chalks or inks, highlighted with oil crayons, or just kissed with mica-based watercolors on the raised patterning.

EMBOSSING INK

A slow-drying clear or tinted ink, used as the wetting agent to hold embossing powder to paper, prior to heating.

EMBOSSING POWDER

A clear or colored plastic resin powder that, when heated, produces a shiny raised image. Available in a variety of colors and metallics, it comes in three grains—fine, suitable for detailed imagery; regular, for everyday stamping; and coarse, used for other creative techniques outside of stamping. *See also* Melt Art, Stamping, and Thermography.

EMBOSSING TINSEL

Embossing powder containing metallic tinsel or a metal glitter product.

EMBROIDERY

A type of ornamental needlework, often on fabric and paper, produced either by hand or by machine.

HOW-TO BASICS: **EMBROIDERY**

Either use a pre-made pattern, or draw your own using pencil dots. Use various threads, lightweight yarns, and beads to embroider easy geometric or floral designs.

Embroidered card

ENCAPSULATION

Placing an element such as paper or other memorabilia in an envelope, between layers of mica, or between two sheets of transparent polyester film, and sealing the sheets together. This method protects an element from damage caused by handling, moisture, and contact with acidic material.

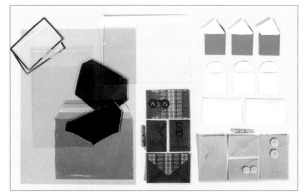

Encapsulation supplies

Mica Tiles are not only a natural and creative addition to cards, but also ideal for encapsulating flowers and other fragile items, protecting them from breakage or leaching color onto the card stock.

An old photo is sandwiched between sepia-colored Mica Tiles encapsulating it. Mounting onto an inked and bleached background provides the old print with the perfect background.

Two pieces of clear vinyl are machine stitched and stuffed with colorful beads, buttons, and embellishments.

ENCAUSTIC

A painting medium in which pigment is suspended in a binder of wax.

HOW-TO BASICS: **ENCAUSTIC**

Using a flat-bottomed iron, heat the wax on a glossy card stock. Use the edge of the iron to drag color, moving it to reveal the white of the paper. This technique produces very organic designs, even designs pretty enough to frame.

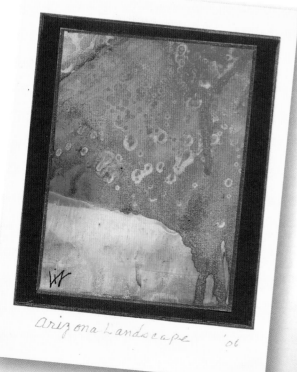

Encaustic card

ENVELOPE

A paper pocket used for covering and mailing cards and letters.

It's not only fun to make your own envelopes, but also a great way to recycle paper. Using an envelope template, available in nearly every size and configuration, gives a whole new creative twist when thinking green.

TIPS FOR ADDRESSING ENVELOPES

- Write legibly, so as not to confuse the optical reading equipment.

- Always use the ZIP/postal code.

- When using software to print addresses, always print the barcodes whenever possible.

- Use simple fonts, such as Arial or Helvetica, and a font size over 12 points.

- Avoid using any graphics in the address zone, as it may confuse the optical reader.

- For formal address, write titles on the envelope, such as "Mr. John Smith" or "Mr. and Mrs. John Smith." Less formally, write "John Smith" or "John and Mary Smith."

- With professionals, use "Dr. and Mrs. John Smith," not "John Smith, M.D., and Mrs. Smith."

- If both the husband and the wife are doctors: "The Doctors Smith."

- If one spouse is a doctor and the other is not: "Mr. John Smith and Dr. Mary Smith."

- When military rank is an issue, the higher rank comes before the lower rank, such as "Major Louise Stover and Lieutenant John Stover."

- If a couple is not married but shares an address, use two lines. Do not add an "and":
  > Ms. Hattie Curtis
  > Mr. Arthur DeMar

- Otherwise, try to get the addressee's name all on one line. When the husband has an unusually long name, indent the wife's title and name on a second line:
  > The Honorable James Henry Churchill and
  > Mrs. James Churchill

EPHEMERA

Printed items produced with the intent of conveying content of some importance to an era, but which are then discarded or recycled. Ephemera can include newspapers, magazines, cigar wrappers, fruit crate labels, ticket stubs, match covers, invitations, pages from books—nearly anything printed, including greeting cards themselves. "Ephemera" is from the Greek word meaning "that which lasts but for a day."

A plethora of ephemera

A pretty floral party napkin holds just the right memories and is the perfect paper ephemera to use when making and sending your hostesses thank you cards.

The Encyclopedia of Greeting Card Tools & Techniques

ETIQUETTE

Practices, rules, and manners to help others feel comfortable. Greeting card rules of etiquette are simple, yet when followed provide a sense of style and tradition.

TIPS

- The proper way to place a card into an envelope is to insert the folded side first and the design face-up, toward the flap.

- If your family creates a holiday newsletter, send it only to family and friends.

- Greeting cards for family and friends may be casual in appearance, but for business, even when handmade, they should have a more professional appearance.

- Send a card to everyone who sends you one.

- Thank-you cards should be sent within one to two weeks after you receive the gift.

- Always include your return address on the envelope.

- Hand-writing an envelope is more personal, and preferable, to using computerized address labels.

- Give children special pens and stickers to decorate their envelopes.

- Check your spelling.

- Sending e-cards is an immediate way to say thanks; however, they should still be followed up with a hand-written card or note.

- E-mailed greeting cards are not a substitute for actual holiday cards.

EYELET

A metal, plastic, or rubber ring or grommet that, when inserted into a hole and flattened, reinforces the hole. Also used as decorative accents in card making, eyelets come in dozens of styles and colors.

EYELET SETTER

A tool for fastening eyelets.

HOW-TO BASICS: **EYELET SETTING**

1. Begin by punching a hole into your card, using a hole punch the same size or slightly smaller than the desired eyelet.

2. Set the eyelet into the hole and turn the card over. From the backside, set the eyelet setter onto the small aperture and tap the end of the setter with a hammer. Continue tapping until the eyelet is flattened into a rounded circle.

FATHER'S DAY CARD

A card sent to your father, grandfather, stepfather, and father figure. Here are a couple of samples to inspire you to create your own. *See also* Holiday Celebration Card.

A paper-folded (origami) collar and tie, adhered to a decorative but more masculine card stock, looks just like a plaid shirt any dad would be proud to wear!

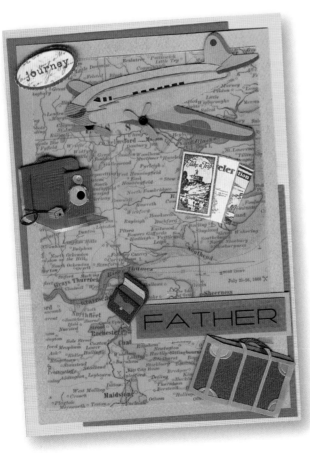

FIBER

A textile material, such as modern yarn and embroidery threads, that is a trendy technique for decorating paper and card stock.

Ribbon, mesh, yarn, twine, and embroidery floss—just some of the fibers you can incorporate into a greeting card.

FLITTER

A mass-production process in which glitter is affixed to produce an iridescent or multi-colored sparkling effect.

FLOWER

Any dry, pressed, preserved paper, silk, or plastic leaves and flowers in card making.

Flowers and leaves can be purchased or pressed and stored inside old telephone books. The Microfleur offers a fast way to preserve summer flowers for instant use.

Tiny flower parts are adhered with PPA-Matte to preserve the color. Placed over stamped or drawn stems, it is a fast and pretty card, useful for any occasion.

While not technically a flower, this pressed skeletonized leaf provides the autumnal feeling needed for this colorful card. The acrylic painted background was sprayed with webbing spray, unifying the multi-colored background.

If I had a single flower for every time I think about you, I could walk forever in my garden.

Claudia Ghandi

FLUSH

Typeset copy that is vertically aligned at the left or right margin.

FOAM STAMP

A foam image adhered to a foam block, this stamp is ideal for fabric stamping and stamping bolder images on textured paper. Foam stamp designs have a more graphic, less detailed look. Foam stamps generally are much less expensive than wood-handled stamps. *See also* Stamping.

Foam stamps provide a certain look that translates well on a greeting card.

FOIL

A metallic, plastic-like material applied to paper using a heat-set method, hot stamping, or with adhesives using pressure. Foil comes in rolls or sheets and a multitude of colors.

FOILING

The art of applying foil to paper or card stock to form words, lines, patterns, borders, or to enhance imagery.

Just as easy as foil tape, shiny rub-on foil is applied to dry tacky Duo adhesive or double-sided tape. After burnishing it down, leaving the edges less than perfect, add layers of paper and a focal point.

Adhesive-backed foil tape is simple to apply and imparts a metallic frame feature for a strong focal image.

FONT

The complete set of characters in a type style.

FOUND OBJECT

An item that exists for another purpose but is altered or incorporated into an object of art.

Found objects can come from anywhere: your backyard, a city street, the beach, a crafts store, a garage sale, or even (gasp!) the trash.

Look for found objects anytime. It's especially fun when vacationing, to add to cards sent to family and friends. Whether it is a smashed bottle cap, oxidized with subtle colors, or a starfish from the beach, found objects add interest and texture to cards.

Even a twig from the garden and a broken frog earring, when placed together with natural colors, textures, and subject matter, will make this card a forever-keeper.

FOXING

Brown spots of what appears to be mildew in the paper's surface is actually fungus. Penetrating the paper, it cannot be removed by erasing, but occasionally may be removed using bleaching techniques.

FRAKTUR

A greeting card, usually a Valentine, with ornamental lettering in the style of illuminated manuscripts from the Middle Ages. Current day frakturs often exhibit a charm and primitive style of hand-cut letters.

FRAME

A geometric or free-form shape or structure surrounding a decorative aspect of the card, enhancing the area.

Frames highlight whatever they contain. They're fun, too!

FRAMING

To enclose in a frame. Sometimes handmade cards are worthy of framing because the sender made a special effort to make a card just for you.

TIPS FOR FRAMING CARDS

- As soon as a card is received, mark on the back: the artist, the date received, and the reason for the card.

- Measure cards immediately and make a shopping list of frame sizes you will need, picking them up as you find them. Every room in the house can have a piece of original art.

- When framed, the message portion of the card can be removed and mounted on the back of the art. For future reference, the date and artist's name are on the back of each framed piece.

GILDING

The art of applying gold, silver, or other metal leaf to a surface.

Gilding comes in many colors including gold, silver, copper, and beautiful metallic variegated colors.

HOW-TO BASICS:
APPLYING GILDING TO CARDS

1. Stamp using gilding adhesive and sponge. When dry, add gilding or glistening metallic pigment.

2. Sponges with varying textures can be used to produce droplet effects. Use gilding adhesive and when dry, add gilding or pigment.

3. Paint on gilding adhesive, as you would watercolor. When dry, add gilding.

4. Create a faux lace using Great Tape. Apply and then nearly rub off the tape. Apply gilding and pigment for a unique bordering or embellishing technique.

5. Add a few drops of leafing adhesive to a Fine Liner, and you've got a great way to write with adhesive. It's gorgeous when gilded with pigments or leafing. Be sure to wash the tool well with liquid soap and water.

GLUE STICK

A round stick of solid glue used to adhere paper to paper. Glue sticks are extremely easy to use; however, as an adhesive for paper crafts, they have a relatively short adhering life expectancy. *See also* Adhesive.

GOUACHE WATERCOLOR

Opaque watercolor containing a colored pigment with a gum binder and an opaque filler. *See also* Watercolor.

GRADUATION CARD

When a friend or loved one graduates, whether it's from a prestigious university or from kindergarten, send a little handmade card to let them know it's a special day. Here are some samples to help get you started. *See also* Special Occasion Card.

The beauty of watercolor is that it can be done nearly any time or any place with few materials. This small study was painted as a tribute to the artist Charles Reid.

GRAIN

The direction in which most fibers in paper run, as a result of the papermaking process. Paper tears more easily with the grain than against it. For some paper varieties, folds made parallel to the grain cause less damage and create smoother, less bulky folds.

GREETING CARD ASSOCIATION

The trade organization representing greeting card and stationery publishers, as well as allied members of the industry. Formed in the U.S. in 1941 in response to a War Department order during World War II to reduce paper use by 25 percent, the Greeting Card Association has evolved over the years since. In 1988, it initiated the Louie awards to celebrate creative excellence in the industry.

GUIDELINES FOR SUBMITTING CARDS

See Card Submission.

GUM ARABIC

A water-soluble gum obtained from the acacia tree and used in lithographic processes. Also, an acid-free powder or liquid binder used to make watercolors.

Two brands of gum arabic

HOT GLUE

An adhesive that is applied in a liquid form while hot, and adheres and hardens as it cools. *See also* Adhesive.

Use a hot glue gun like a paintbrush, dispensing hot liquid glue into interesting abstract or representative drawings. Just before it cools completely, carefully place flat pieces of gilding or dust on mica pigments. When completely cool, use a textured sponge to remove any extra particles.

HOT-PRESSED PAPER

A smooth, glazed paper surface produced by rolling and pressing a finished sheet of paper through hot metal cylinders. *See also* Paper.

HUFFING

Exhaling on an inked stamp image to keep it moist before stamping. This process can extend the ink to allow a second impression without re-inking.

ILLUMINATION

Illuminated letters were usually, but not exclusively, the first letter of a page or paragraph, enlarged and embellished with gold and brilliant color, often incorporating and intertwining among the letter itself, various animals, plants, and mythological creatures.

Both of these cards show illuminated letters drawn using a Fine Liner with Duo. When dry, the 'A' was enhanced using sparkling dry mica pigments, and the 'B' using gilding leaf.

Ink Pad

A clear or colored ink-soaked pad used to wet the stamp, then the paper. *See also* Stamping.

Interference

Paint or pigment that contains mica particles combined with pigment or dye to achieve an overall iridescent, pearlescent, or metallic appearance. *See also* Mica.

Interference Mica

Tiny, transparent mica flakes, coated on all sides with a thin layer of metal oxide—either iron oxide or titanium dioxide—that is highly refractive and reflective simultaneously. The thickness of the metal oxide layer determines the size of the light wavelength, which determines the color of the iridescence. The pearlescent quality when used as a watercolor is particularly brilliant on a dark background. *See also* Mica.

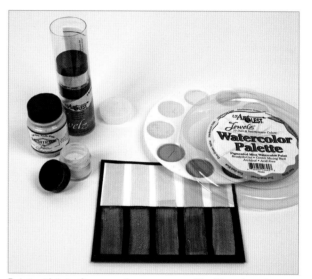

Paint with interference mica as you would with watercolors.

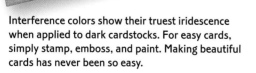

Interference colors show their truest iridescence when applied to dark cardstocks. For easy cards, simply stamp, emboss, and paint. Making beautiful cards has never been so easy.

Apply peel-off gold stickers to card stock, using both the positive and negative shapes. Fill in the areas using the interference watercolors. Cut and assemble each square to resemble a mosaic tile floor.

Using interference watercolor paints with watercolor markers enlarges the color choices for card makers. It is also a terrific way to learn about shading and color. The markers and watercolors will work on any dark or light surface.

INVITATION

A card that invites the recipient to an event or special occasion. A close cousin to the greeting card, an invitation should match the style of the event. *See also* Invitation Card.

INVITATION TIPS

- Always include the following:
  - Name of the host or hostess
  - Purpose of the invitation (birthday party, wedding, holiday, etc.) or name of the person to be honored
  - Day, date, and time of the event
  - Location of the event (street address, city and state, but no ZIP code)
  - Appropriate attire
- Proofread your invitation for mistakes and forgotten information.
- Formal invitations require eight weeks' advance notice.
- Try to send out informal invitations at least four weeks in advance.

This quilled invitation to a bridal shower is both personalized and a forever keepsake.

MANDALA

An ornamental stamp or pattern of Hindu origin, which when cut and layered resembles a decorative, dimensional, lace-like design.

Mandala template

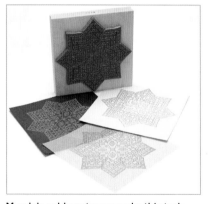

Mandala rubber stamps make this technique easy. Simply stamp an image several times and layer the images, as shown in these examples, to form the mandala.

MARBLING

A technique of applying patterns, resembling marble textures, to paper. *See also* Paper.

Marbling using melted embossing powder

Watercolor-painted marbling

MARKER

A pen or brush-like device holding solvent or water-based ink, watercolor, or paint. *See also* Pen.

Apply watercolor markers directly to a rubber stamp. Apply all the colors simultaneously. Right before stamping, huff onto the stamp several times to moisten the watercolor, and then stamp.

Stamp and emboss the images and use watercolor markers to color in the image. The markers will not show on the embossing powder.

MASKING

A technique using tape or paper, whereby covering specific areas, while stamping or painting images appear behind or in front of one another, creating a dimensional effect.

While frosted vellum is de-emphasizing the finished image, note how the frog is actually in front of the grass, instead of behind.

1. Stamp an image using any ink product on the top side of sticky notepaper. Try to stamp so that most of the image covers the sticky part. Cut the image out completely. (This is your mask.)

2. Stamp the same image on your card and use watercolor markers or other coloring devices to enhance the image.

3. Cover the stamped image on your card with the mask from step 1 and stamp other images over the top. (The sticky part will help hold the mask in place during this creative process.) Remove the mask.

You can duplicate and figure out the many layers of masking by deconstructing this card image. Use multiple masks in several shapes, including cut-outs of the actual stamped image and scraps of square paper.

Torn scraps of computer paper appear as mountainous regions. Sponge with ink or chalk each layer to form the desert landscape.

MAT BOARD

A heavy fiberboard used to protect artwork or as a hard art-making surface. It is available in a wide variety of colors and textures.

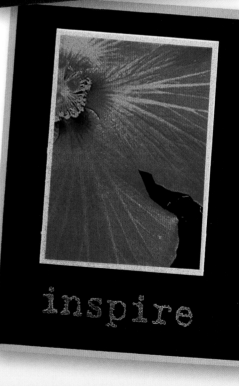

Both of these cards were made using laser-printed acetate photos. When applied to metallic mat-board pieces, they provide an interesting multi-layered focal point.

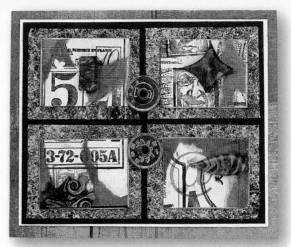

Suze Weinberg,
Melt Art

An internationally celebrated rubber-stamp artist, Suze Weinberg began designing and creating with rubber stamps more than 18 years ago. While Suze may have started stamping as a hobby, she has since spent many years developing unique products for the rubber-stamp industry, including Ultra Thick Embossing Enamel, Wonder Tape, The Melting Pot, BeaDazzles, Mold 'n Pour, and dozens of others.

Suze is recognized not only as one of the founders of the American rubber stamp movement, but also for her expertise in develping the techniques of melt art. Both skills translate into wonderful greeting cards. Known for her years of product education, development, and editorial contributions, she also delivers an always informative and fun "Schmooze With Suze" newsletter and website (www.schmoozewithsuze.com).

Suze continues to write books, produce videos, and travel the world teaching techniques using the products that bear her name, all the while exploring new adventures, such as photography and computer technology. Taking a class or workshop with Suze is both a comedic and creatively joyful experience, as she teaches using humor mingled with expertise.

MEMORABILIA

A collection of remembrances, such as bits of paper ephemera or personal items that remind you of a special time, place, thing, or event.

Memorabilia card

MESH

A material characterized by its open, net-like appearance. Mesh may be made of fabric, jute, paper, or plastic. It's a popular textural element in card making.

METAL ART

A decoration made from various metals, including tin, pewter, or copper or other metal-like substances using aging patinas, and techniques such as embossing, debossing, repoussé, and etching.

Using a vinyl copper-colored sticker and metal mesh, begin by heating the mesh with a heat gun to alter the color. Apply the sticker and cut the entire image out. Use the mounting squares to raise the image, adhering it to a stamped and painted background.

A tin elephant coated with silver embossing powder is layered onto a marbled polymer sun and stamped background. Cut-outs of grass and Mica Flakes add even more texture and just the right finishing details.

Ready-made molds or even rubber stamps can be used to provide a surface for creating textural metal borders, such as the one on "Mona Lisa Smile" or the focal point, such as on the "Heartfelt Wishes" card. To enhance the raised or debossed areas, use acrylic glazes, waxes, and hammered backgrounds using a small nail or tool. The background for "Copper Potter" was accomplished using an embossing stylus.

Mica

A transparent, flaky mineral with excellent heat-resistance, characterized by the formation of thin-layered sheets. Mica color ranges from colorless to black. When used with paint or attached to other pigments, it produces a wide range of iridescent, pearlescent, or metallic products. Colored mica particles and flakes are used as embellishments. *See also* Interference Mica.

Stamp and emboss a Mica Tile, using a large image such as this tulip stamp. From the reverse side, apply clear drying PPA-Gloss. In sections, apply the glue and Mica D'Lights. Then turn the tile over, revealing the finished "stained glass window" effect. Adhere the tile to a card, using a bit of shiny fiber for even more sparkle.

Adhered with a clear acrylic adhesive, larger bits of mica when colored appear as textural, glimmering, miniature brushstrokes of paint.

Both of these cards have been stenciled with artist cement. The wet image is sprinkled with tiny mica bits. It's much like glitter, though the mica's appearance is more subtly sparkling.

Apply a vinyl sticker to card stock and cut it out. Simply apply clear-drying PPA-Gloss, and Mica D'Lights or Glitter to the inside sections. Apply that over a colorful background and use vinyl hinges for further embellishing.

daisy

Thank You

159

MONOCHROMATIC

See Color.

MONTAGE

A composite art piece made by cutting or tearing photos, then adhering them together to produce a homogenous whole.

Montage card

MOSAIC

The papercraft technique of cutting or tearing similar or disparate paper and reassembling them to create a new image.

Congratulations

MOTHER'S DAY CARD

One of the most popular holidays in the world for sending a card, Mother's Day has a rich history of giving handmade cards. Remember when you made a card at school to bring home? Now you're older, wiser, and much more skilled. Make a special card to show your mother how much she means to you. Here are some samples.

Stamp, emboss, and paint a butterfly on very thick card stock. When cut, the card stock can be smoothed over your fingers, rounding and raising the wings. Collage torn Mica Tiles, Gossamer Fibers, and small letters to create the sentiment. This is a card your mom will always treasure.

MOULD

A flat screen with wire mesh onto which the deckle is placed during hand-paper making.

MOULD MADE

A sheet of paper that simulates the look of handmade paper but is actually made by a machine called a cylinder mould. *See also* Handmade Paper.

MOUNT

To adhere a photograph, embellishment, or other item to another piece of paper.

MOUNTAIN FOLD

See Accordion Folding and Valley Fold.

MOUNTED STAMP

The block of wood or acrylic used as a handle that provides stability of the die when stamping. *See also* Stamping.

MOVEABLE CARD

A card that incorporates a mechanical element, such as a pull-tab, pop-up component, or makes use of ingenious folding techniques providing the illusion of movement as the card opens. Also called interactive or engineered cards. *See also* Transformation.

This moveable 'vovelle' reveals a greeting and several images by rotating the wheel engineered to move behind the window.

A BRIEF HISTORY OF THE MOVEABLE CARD

The first known interactive paper element dates back to the 13th century. Books called vovelles contained a paper disc placed on a central pivot that, when rotated, revealed or pointed to words or symbols on the page. These books had become popular with children by 1880 when "metamorphoses" books, also called turn-up books, included fold-out illustrations. The moveable card art form reached a peak during that time. The cards combined the various mechanical processes with highly detailed embossed parts, making pop-up, vovelles, or transformations into elaborately colorful greeting cards. Transformations are a type of moveable card that show a scene made up of vertical slats. By pulling a tab on the side, the slats slide under and over one another to "transform" into a totally different scene.

MULBERRY PAPER

See Paper and Washi Paper.

MYLAR

A protective clear covering for photos and cards. Mylar is currently regarded as the highest quality material used for this purpose.

NEW BABY CARD

A card sent to celebrate a birth. New parents are usually overwhelmed, but always appreciate a thoughtful card. Make it a handmade card and surprise them. Here are some samples to show you several different approaches.

Congratulations

Tiny paper-quilled footprints are nearly as perfect as the real thing!

B A B Y

NEW YEAR'S CARD

While you might not think of New Year's Eve and New Year's Day as normal card-giving holidays, think of all the possibilities—new beginnings, resolutions, reminders, and just plain fun. Here is one fun idea for a card; there are many more throughout the book.

1. Begin this simple design, following the pattern and using your bone folder to make crisp folds.

2. Finish each heart, using various colors of red and patterned papers to create more interest in design and texture.

Notice the strong composition of this card, with its bold shapes and added geometry of fiber elements. The playful curvilinear line of the hearts gives this card its appeal.

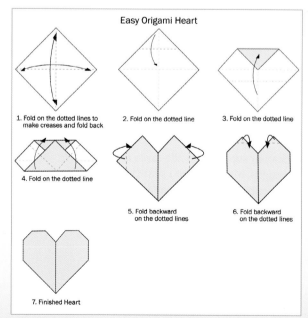

Easy Origami Heart

1. Fold on the dotted lines to make creases and fold back

2. Fold on the dotted line

3. Fold on the dotted line

4. Fold on the dotted line

5. Fold backward on the dotted lines

6. Fold backward on the dotted lines

7. Finished Heart

Dozens of free origami patterns (like this one) are available online and in books. Follow some of the simpler patterns for cardmaking and assemble them as shown.

ORNARE

A technique in which a decorative template is placed on the reverse side of card stock, then pierced completely or partially through, using a pin or needle tool.

OVAL CUTTER

A specialized paper trimmer that cuts paper or photographs into oval shapes.

Ornare cards

P

PAINT

An art material made of pigment and binder. Pigment provides color to paint, and in its raw form it is ground. *See also* Acrylic Paint, Gouache Watercolor, Mica Watercolor, Specialty Paint, Watercolor.

Paint for greeting cards is made by many different manufacturers in an almost endless array of colors.

Acrylic painted card

PAPER

A material made of vegetable fibers composed of cellulose held together by hydrogen bonding. The most common source of paper fiber is wood pulp, but may also include cotton, hemp, linen, flax, and rice. *See also* Card Stock, Coated Paper Stock, Corrugated Paper, Embossed Paper, Paste Paper, Permanent Paper, Photo Paper, Printed Paper, Ready-Made Card Stock, Sticker Paper, Tissue, Vellum, Washi Paper, and Watercolor Paper.

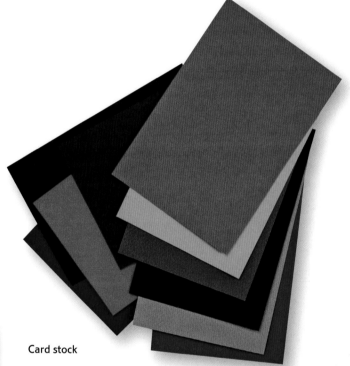

Card stock

Metallic papers

Paper is one of the most important design and compositional elements in cardmaking, so familiarize yourself with the variety available. Paper selections may offer more or less texture, bright or subtle whites and color tones, as well as various levels of opacity or translucency. Each paper type has very individual characteristics. Besides how the paper accepts the paint, markers, stampings, or stenciling, or how it cuts or ages, it is the actual surface of the paper that can make or break a card design. Select the main stock of a card that texturally relates to the overall theme and other materials you will be using.

Printed papers

Handmade papers

Lace paper/Washi paper

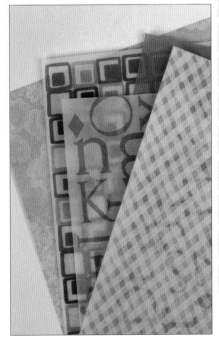

Vellum

PAPER CASTING

A method of using pulp and a mold to create a shaped paper card feature.

Paper casting can produce some amazing results. Try it and see!

Paper casting is fun, inexpensive, and easy. Simply mix recycled paper, cotton linter, or cotton sheets in a blender, or soak a few tissues in a cup of water to make a slushy pulp. Press it into a ready-made or custom-made polymer clay mold, and then allow it to dry.

1. Spray molds with a cooking oil product to prevent sticking.

2. Apply wet pulp to the mold, using your fingers.

3. Pat the pulp using a clean sponge, removing air bubbles and excess water.

4. Use a firm bristle brush to further tamp the pulp into the mold's details.

5. Allow the castings to dry in the mold naturally.

6. Use a thin tool (like a dinner knife) to carefully ease, first the edges, then the casting itself, from the mold. If the casting is not fully formed, rehydrate it in the blender, and start again.

7. Save the excess pulp in the freezer in an airtight container for future use.

8. Embellish dried castings with watercolor, pastels, or markers, and then adhere them to a card.

Cards with paper-casting elements

PAPER CUTTER

Any tool or device that cuts paper. Dozens of choices are available, but the tools recommended for card making are: a large pair of scissors for general cutting; a small pair of scissors for detail work; a craft knife, mat, and metal ruler; a small guillotine paper cutter; and a paper trimmer.

PAPER CUTTING

A distinctive Chinese handicraft, originating from the 6th century when women pasted gold- and silver-colored foil cuttings in their hair, and men used them in sacred rituals. Later, paper cuttings became more colorful and were used during festivals to decorate gates and windows. *See also* Scherenschnitte.

A paper-cut card

PAPER DOLL CARD

A greeting card made from a die-cut image in the shape of a person or containing the components for making a paper doll.

Paper doll greeting cards were once charming to give and more delightful to receive. This one from the Willimantic Thread Co. was one of the earliest paper doll advertisements, and folded into thirds to fit into an envelope.

Unique paper doll cards

PAPER ENAMELING

A technique in which the acrylic glossy product Perfect Paper Adhesive (PPA) is poured over artwork, such as paper collage, to form a thick opaque layer. When completely dry, the layer becomes crystal clear with a glass-like finish, resulting in artwork that resembles copper enameling. The technique was developed and the term coined by the author.

A paper-enameled card

PAPER FASTENER

Any utilitarian or decorative fastener made to hold card-making elements in place.

PAPER FOLDING

See Accordion Folding, Fold Out Card, and Moveable Card.

PAPER TRIMMER

A tool that works by aligning paper to a grid and sliding the small, razor-like blade on the built-in track, cutting the paper in a single movement.

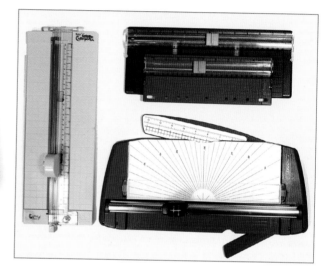

PAPER WEAVING

A technique of weaving paper strips in a method similar to weaving fibers. *See also* Weaving.

Papuela

The technique of inserting thin paper strips through slotted paper to create a woven-like pattern.

A papuela card

Parchment Craft

Embossing, scoring, or piercing translucent paper, often vellum, to create delicate lace-like patterns. Also called pergamano.

Paste

See Adhesive.

Paste Paper

A method of altering, texturing, and decorating a plain or patterned paper surface using one of several kinds of paint and common hand tools. *See also* Paper.

Paste paper is often prettier than a printed paper because it provides reflective texture. The process of making the paper is a pleasurable art form and one any card maker can enjoy, using acrylic paints, glazes, and traditional paste recipes.

TIP

Making paste paper can be a messy, but fun art form. Invite lots of friends and make a day of it. Have everyone make one style and then swap, increasing each person's stash of colored and textured papers for card making.

The Encyclopedia of Greeting Card Tools & Techniques

	HOW-TO BASICS: **PASTE PAPER**	

Paste Ingredients

Yield: 1 pint (2 cups) of paste

2 cups warm water
1 tablespoon methyl cellulose,
   rice starch, or cake flour

Creating the Paste

1. Pour 1 cup of the water into a medium-sized bowl and sprinkle in the methyl cellulose. Stir well. Set aside to thicken for about 1 to 2 hours, stirring occasionally.

2. Add up to ¾ cup more warm water, stirring until thoroughly blended. The mixture should be the consistency of unset pudding. If it is too thick, add up to ¼ cup more water.

3. Divide the mixture into several cups, depending on how many colors you want to use for your papers, and add approximately (you'll need to experiment) 1 tablespoon of color to each cup. Tempera, acrylic, gouache, inks, or dry pigments (matte or iridescent) all work well for color.

4. Store the unused portions in covered containers and refrigerate.

Application

1. Choose paper that is relatively smooth, not too absorbent, but able to withstand being wet—watercolor, recycled, or bond papers, for example.

2. For paler tones, dampen and relax the paper. For more intense colors, omit this step.

3. After you have applied the colors, use sponges, combs, carved plastic applicators, or brushes to make various designs in the paste. Set the papers aside to dry.

4. When the papers are completely dry, iron them from the back on several layers of newspaper. Do not use steam.

PASTEL

A squared or rounded stick of color, consisting of ground colored pigment and a binder. The pigments used in pastels are the same as those used to produce all paint. Pastels used in card making must be protected with a fixative.

Pastel crayons and pencils

TYPES OF PASTELS

- **Soft pastels** contain a higher percentage of binder to pigment, providing a greater ease of blending.

- **Hard pastels** contain a higher percentage of pigment to binder, providing a firmer and more defined drawing texture and detail.

- **Pastel pencils** are available in both a soft and hard pastel, encased in a wooden stick handle much like any pencil. These are ideal for artists with sensitivities to handling pigments or binders. Pastel pencils may be sharpened, and they produce less dust than traditional pastels.

- **Oil pastels** feature an oil binder and produce intense colors, though they are more difficult to blend.

With pastels, you can blend colors before you seal them with a fixative.

PHOTO CORNER

A self-adhesive paper triangle or decorative shape, used for mounting and easy removal of photographs or memorabilia.

Mica is very versatile and can even be die-cut to form mounting corners and give a card composition a translucent organic design element. Naturally sepia-toned sparkling mica bits sprinkled onto embossing paste work well with mica corners.

PHOTO MOUNTING CORNER

A self-adhesive polypropylene, metal, plastic, or other material, often with a triangle-like shape, used for decoratively mounting a card element or photograph.

Photo mounting products have progressed way past basic black.

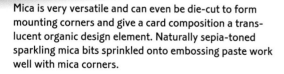

from one glamorous babe to another!

A card with metal photo mounting corners

The Encyclopedia of Greeting Card Tools & Techniques

PHOTO PAPER

Paper made especially for inkjet or laser printing. Select photo paper for its brightness, weight, and finish. *See also* Paper.

PHOTO TAPE

A usually archival quality, permanent, self-adhesive tape with an easy-to-remove paper backing—also called a liner.

PHOTO TINTING

The technique of lightly applying color to a black-and-white or sepia-colored photograph, by using oil or other specialty water-soluble paints or markers. Besides the traditional photo-tinting techniques, much of the process can be accomplished today using the computer. Computer-generating photos and enhancing them mechanically can produce interesting and colorful results.

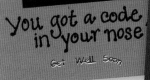

Examples of tinted photo cards

PIERCING

Pricking paper with a needle or needle-like tool for the purpose of creating a punched pattern. *See also* Ornare.

PIGMENT

A non-water soluble substance used to color ink, paint, paper, and textiles. Natural organic pigments are generally more stable than dyes, but produce a narrower color selection. *See also* Paint.

POCKET CARD

A card with a pocket added to or constructed into it.

Pocket cards can offer surprises of all kinds. This card holds a half-dozen mini-stick puppets. What child wouldn't like this in their Halloween sack?

Other pocket cards hold tags with the card's message.

The Encyclopedia of Greeting Card Tools & Techniques

POLISHED STONE

A paper coloring technique using permanent solvent-based ink, denatured alcohol, and gilding markers made by Krylon. When the ink is drizzled onto glossy or metallic card stock, dotted with the marker, and then blended with alcohol, the finished paper resembles polished marble. This technique and term, developed by artist Suze Weinberg, is often imitated using various other art materials, but seldom looks quite as spectacular.

TIP

Begin by having a play day! Spend time making piles of polished stone papers, keeping even those that seem less than successful. Use them to stamp on, making them into layered card borders or even into serendipity cards.

This card, covered with a stamped and inked piece of frosty vellum, showcases the brilliant polished stone technique and the interesting compositional juxtaposition of matte and glossy textures.

Simply stamped and embossed with gold powder, then mounted and corner-punched, this card was a favorite of all those who recieved it.

Spend some time experimenting with polished stone and resist techniques. The results are stunning and memorable cards.

POLYMER CLAY

A modeling material composed of resin, plasticizer, and occasional filler. Colorful, permanent, and water-resistant, polymer clay cures at a temperature of 265°F. It remains flexible when rolled thin and used for card making elements. *See also* Clay.

POLYVINYL ACETATE (PVA)

A vinyl polymer used in adhesive. Commonly called white glue or PVA, it is a safe adhesive as shown by its widespread use in schools. Bond time is immediate, although the tackier versions of PVA can take up to several hours to dry thoroughly. Dry time also depends on the thickness of application and the products being adhered. *See also* Adhesive.

Polymer clay cards

POP-UP CARD

A foldable greeting card, which in the folded position is relatively flat and fits into an ordinary mailing envelope. The front or inside of the card displays a decorative section that self-generates a three-dimensional, pop-up structure when the card is opened. *See also* Moveable Card.

While you can construct pop-up cards entirely by hand, manufacturers have produced products such as Popeze. This material is cut, made into a box shape, and applied to the card. A sticker, applied to a background paper, is the beginning of a pop-up.

Jane Gill,
Punch Craft

Stamping happened quite by accident for Jane Gill. "Working on a piece of furniture, I went to a craft shop to buy some paint. They happened to have an amazing stamping demonstration that weekend, so I bought some of their products, thinking it would work for my furniture." After showing her finished work to the shop owner, he wisely asked Jane to begin teaching.

Like many artists, that first stamping experience led Jane from one medium to another. She eventually gravitated toward greeting cards.

A meeting with Leone Em, the leading Australian designer of punch craft, inspired Jane to try that particular art form. It was a natural fit for Jane, who found she could tap into her formal education in botanical and natural history illustration to design punch craft flowers.

Jane graciously shares her ideas and inspires others by demonstrating and teaching around the United Kingdom. She says, "I'm very lucky to be able to use my talents in so many media, from furniture design to watercolor, from rubber stamping to paper crafting."

P

PUNCHIE

The paper shape made from using a punch, not the hole itself. Paper crafters use punchies independently of the paper originally punched. In other words, it's a great technique for mixing paper types.

PUZZLE CARD

Preassembled blank card-sized jigsaw puzzle pieces, used to make a greeting card or invitation. Decorated as a solid puzzle and then disassembled, pieces are put into an envelope for mailing, to be reassembled by the recipient. Common from the late 1800s to the early 1900s, puzzle cards—then known as trade cards—were used for advertising. Images were often hidden within a puzzle.

PVA

See Polyvinyl Acetate.

Printed machine-made paper scraps lend themselves to quilting. Piece together even the smallest and narrowest paper scraps to resemble traditional quiltwork.

A narrow piece of fabric quilting is repurposed from the much larger design and fits nicely into a window card. The olive-toned card stock and white card surface provide a balance of color. A fine-tip marker adds a repetitive border design as seen in the fabric. Rub-on type creates the sentiment.

A unique saying, scripture, verse, poem, or memorable word used to express a personal idea or sentiment. A quote can also acknowledge the card recipient's particular occasion. (For a selection of quotes and sentiments, see page 279.)

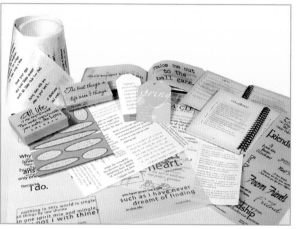

If calligraphy isn't your forte, you can still add nicely designed sentiments to your cards using these products.

RAFFIA

A natural fiber used in card making as an alternative to ribbon, providing a more casual or country appearance.

RAGGED EDGE

Unjustified copy. Usually, this refers to the right side of a paragraph of text.

RAG PAPER OR BOARD

A paper or board manufactured with a high content of long, cotton fibers, often used in high-quality card making.

RAINBOW PAD

A rubber-stamp ink pad with several colors side by side, designed for multi-color stamping and brayer painting.

RANDOM ACT OF KINDNESS

Sending a card or gift to someone anonymously, for no reason.

READY-MADE CARD STOCK

Blank cards and matching envelopes that can be transformed into a card for any occasion. Many ready-made varieties come embossed with borders, foiled with gold edges, or printed with geometrics. *See also* Card Stock and Paper.

Ready-made card stock and envelopes

RECYCLING

The act of reprocessing used or abandoned materials to create something entirely new. For card makers, this includes old greeting cards, paper, ephemera, and other objects.

TIPS

- Scan greeting cards onto your computer and recycle the real card.

- Carefully cut the main image into the shape needed for a craft, or into a tag shape for next year's gifts. Even the sentiment makes a nice gift tag. Throw away the rest of the card.

RED-EYE PEN

A pen specially made to take red-eye out of flash photographs.

REGISTER

The process of positioning two or more images so they are precisely superimposed. *See also* Stamp Positioner.

REINKER

A small bottle of ink made to refill stamp pads. May also be used independently for card making techniques that require wet colorants. Reinkers come in an array of colors and types, such as permanent, water based, hybrid, and solvent ink. *See also* Stamping.

Bits of Christmas wrap saved from year to year can be recycled for all kinds of paper craft projects. Here tiny bits were torn and attached to create a contemporary design. With a sprinkle of glitter or mica flakes, the tree literally glimmers, catching every light beam.

RELIEF EMBOSSING

See Dimensional Embossing.

REPOSITIONABLE ADHESIVE

A pressure-sensitive adhesive with a low tack characteristic, leaving minimal residue, staining, or damage when removed. *See also* Adhesive.

REPURPOSED CARD

A card made by using material that was previously used for another purpose.

Repurposed cards

A FEW VARIETIES OF DESERT CACTI - M 16

REPURPOSING TIPS

- Cut off the front of a card and simply reattach it to a blank card so someone else can enjoy.

- Carefully cut the image and consider how it may look best: mounted onto colored stock, glittered, dimensionalized, or collaged into one to create a theme or quilt-like design.

Repurposing a seed packet into a greeting card gives cardmakers dozens of options. Use just the words, the flower photo, or, like the example, use the whole pack. Give it for any spring holiday or birthday. Or how about forget-me-nots for Mother's Day?

RESIST

A technique that preserves the white area of card stock. There are many techniques to cause paint or paper to resist color, from using wax-based colored pencils to traditional batik methods using paraffin wax and crayons. In addition, there are several liquid masking materials to paint or stamp with, such as Masquepen and Liquid Frisket, embossing powder resists, white glue or PPA (Perfect Paper Adhesive), and watercolor resists. This technique requires experimentation and patience, because often the design does not appear until after you've applied the wash and it has thoroughly dried.

HOW-TO BASICS: RESIST

1. Generously and evenly apply PPA to a piece of Cut 'n Dry. Using it as a stamp pad, stamp an image onto the paper. A shimmering gold card stock was used for this example.

Mix gum arabic and water to form a liquid paste. Stamp it onto glossy card stock and let it dry thoroughly. Sponge on alcohol-based inks. When dry, gently wipe the surface with a damp sponge, removing the gum Arabic. The white of the paper below shines through.

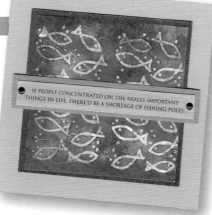

Stamp and emboss with clear ink and embossing powder. Apply inks over the surface, and, if necessary, buff the paper to remove excess ink. The white of the paper shows through the fish, which have resisted the ink.

The bold geometry of this Hot Potatoes stamp really shows off the full potential of the technique.

Apply a Masque Pen, PPA, or Crystal Lacquer to a stamp and press it to the paper. When dry, sponge on watercolors. When dry, buff or remove the masque resist by rubbing it off with your fingers.

2. When the PPA has dried, apply sparkling watercolors over the surface, allowing the colors to intermingle.

3. When completely dry, gently buff the paper with a cotton ball or tissue, revealing understated but beautiful stamped imagery, the gold paper shimmering through.

Another take on the technique also uses shimmering gold paper. This time, the stamp and emboss use clear embossing powder. Sponge a mica-based watercolor paint over the surface. Buff the art when dry, using a soft tissue, revealing perfect butterflies.

Draw a pattern onto watercolor paper using a fine point or paintbrush with PPA or Crystal Lacquer. When dry, apply traditional watercolors and dry. Add in more color using watercolor markers, and spritz the card to encourage the colors to bleed.

Apply stickers to paper and carefully rub stamping inks over the paper. Remove the sticker and apply others, creating multiple layers of design.

RHINESTONE

Though they are artificial gems, rhinestones often have facets that sparkle like a diamond. Originally, rhinestones were rock crystals gathered from the Rhine River in Europe. Today, crystal rhinestones are produced primarily in Austria by Swarovski. Inexpensive glass and plastic rhinestones are used as embellishment in card making.

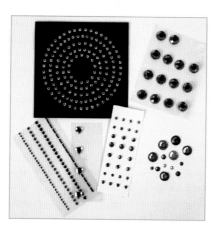

Selecting just the right papers and popping on some sticky-backed rhinestones and dazzle dots makes card making quick, easy, and sparkling!

RIBBON

A narrow strip of fabric, either finished at the edges or left ragged, used for embellishing, trimming, tying, or finishing a card composition.

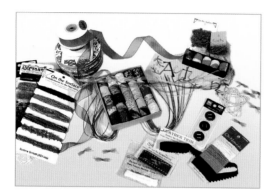

Ready-made adhesive-backed ribbon makes it easy to border window-cards, emphasize a card's greeting, or deck the halls and the tree.

It's Your Day!

ROLLER STAMP

A stamp consisting of a single-strip image mounted on a roller resembling a brayer. When rolled, it provides a continuous image on the stamping surface. *See also* Stamping.

RUBBER STAMP

A hand tool manufactured of rubber, or a rubber-like product, made to reproduce an image onto any surface using paint or ink. A rubber stamp can be used for thousands of impressions. *See also* Stamping.

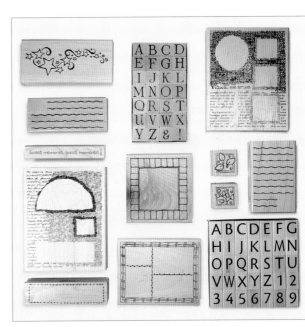

wish

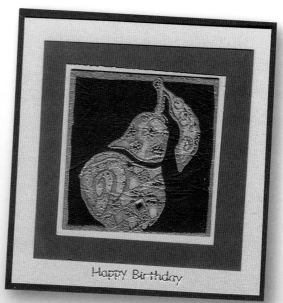

Happy Birthday

Kevin Nakagawa,
Scenic Stamping

Growing up near Vandenberg Air Force Base on the north end of Santa Barbara County, California, Kevin Nakagawa spent his childhood days fishing, clamming, and hunting abalone along the pristine coastline, as well as exploring the oak-filled chaparral with his dad. These experiences laid the groundwork for his career to come.

While attending college, Kevin took a job with A Stamp in the Hand, Co. "It was my first exposure to art rubber stamps, and while I was hired for general production, I ended up with a few hundred designs in their line by the time I graduated from college, and struck out on my own," he says.

Armed with a Bachelor of Fine Arts degree in Illustration and an entrepreneurial spirit, Kevin began working on his own nature-inspired designs, and thus Stampscapes was born.

"In the time that it takes to stamp out a card, I can take a mental micro-vacation to a tropical island at sunset, drop my line into a crystal clear lake at dawn, take a walk through a grove of oak trees, or take a hike at high elevations where we're looking down at the clouds," he says. "Stampscapes has been a culmination of so many experiences and interests. It's been the perfect job, but more than a job, it's become a passion and a teacher of life."

BLUE ICE BY KEVIN NAKAGAWA

Materials and Tools
Stamps (from Stampscapes)
Glossy card stock
Sponge applicators
White gel pen
Spray bottle
Dye-based inks in light blue,
    medium blue, dark blue,
    and black
Pigment ink in white

Instructions

1. Apply the ink from light blue to dark blue, layering each. The lightest colors should cover the entire card, but apply the darker colors on the left and right toward the outside edges only.

2. Apply the ink using a sponge and defined directional strokes, creating a streaky look.

3. When completely inked, lightly spritz the card with water. Where the water lands, the ink will lift, causing a bleached appearance and creating an illusion of deep space.

4. Stamp the foliage in three colors—light blue to create background branches, which will visually recede into the background; medium blue for the middle ground; and dark blue for the foreground.

5. Stamp additional branches using the black dye-based ink.

6. Stamp additional branches using the white pigment ink.

7. For additional details, use the white gel pen for the sky and the tips of the branches. These little dot details create a sparkle and introduce light back into the dark areas.

SCHERENSCHNITTE

(Pronounced *shair-en-shnit-teh*.) A scissor-cutting technique used to decorate birth and marriage certificates and create Christmas decorations. It became a popular folk art form in the 1800s.

Purchased in the Amish country and nearly 45 years old, this Scherenschnitte piece remained in the drawer until just the right moment. Finally mounted onto red card stock, it has been transformed into a charming wedding card.

SCISSORS

A hand tool used to cut paper, card stock, fabric, or other materials. Don't try to make greeting cards without one (or two).

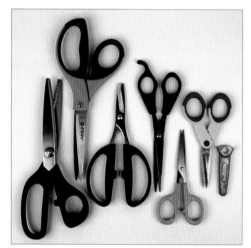

These are scissors every card maker will find useful. From left, they are pinking shears for cutting a fancy edge; shears for cutting card stock and mat board; Kai scissors for fatigue-free cutting; general scissors; children's scissors; and detail scissors with a safety cap.

SCORE

To crease paper with a burnisher or stylus, making it easier to crisply fold paper. Scoring allows card makers to make finished cards using scrap paper and discarded card stock.

HOW-TO BASICS: SCORING

Score your paper before folding it, and you'll get clean, professional-looking cards.

SCRAPBOOK

A blank book in which miscellaneous items such as greeting cards are collected and preserved. *See also* Organization.

SCRATCH ART

A technique of scratching into a surface, revealing the pattern or design underneath.

SCRATCH BOARD

A drawing board coated with white clay and a surface layer of black ink that when scratched or scraped away produces an effect similar to engraving.

Mica Tiles lend themselves to the scratch art technique because of their transparency and ability to receive color.

Glaze mixed with paint and applied to coated glossy stock slows the drying time. Slower drying means there's plenty of time to scratch in even the most intricate design. Use a paintbrush handle or orange stick for this style of card making.

SEALING WAX AND SEAL

A technique of impressing a design into hot wax using a metal die. The resulting disk features a pattern such as an image or letter.

SECONDARY COLOR

See Color.

SELF-HEALING CUTTING MAT

A composite mat designed to allow the use of rotary and straight utility blades without showing marks or cutting lines. Often the mat is printed with pre-calculated grid patterns and angles, making it ideal for designing and cutting card making elements.

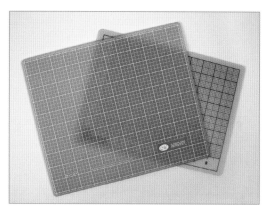

SELF-INKING STAMP

A stamp with an inkpad built into the handle. Commonly found in an office supply store, the tool may also provide uniquely fun words and titles for card makers. *See also* Stamping.

The Encyclopedia of Greeting Card Tools & Techniques

SEPIA COLOR

A dark brown ink or pigment traditionally prepared from the secretion of the cuttlefish, but now replicated using more common materials such as walnut ink, reinkers, paint, and glaze.

SEPIA PRINT

A photograph with a distinctive brown-to-olive-brown tint.

SEQUIN

A small, shiny ornamental disk, usually made of plastic, used for card making ornamentation and embellishing.

SERENDIPITY

A cardmaking technique in which handmade, collaged, stamped, inked, or pre-printed patterned papers are cut into geometric shapes, such as strips, squares, rectangles, and then randomly reassembled into different patterns and directions.

Serendipity cards

SHADOW STAMPING

A technique using color on a large, flat rubberstamp image that becomes the background composition for a focal point. *See also* Stamping.

Stamp with ink or paint and then add embellishments.

SHAKER CARD

A card making construction technique similar to a shakable snow globe. A shaker card usually is made with two or three layers: a decorative background; an acetate covered box; a cellophane envelope or other clear container containing "shakable" embellishments such as glitter, charms, and beads; and possibly a decorative top layer.

A shaker card

Examples of shadow stamping

SHAVING CREAM OR STARCH PAPER MARBLING

A technique for faux marbling paper using a liquid colorant and shaving cream or liquid starch.

1. Fill a shallow pan with about 1 inch of shaving cream. Level the cream with a ruler or paint stick.

2. Randomly drop two or three colors of liquid acrylic paint, stamp pad ink, or food coloring onto the shaving cream. Use a toothpick, the back end of a paint brush, or a texture tool to gently distribute the color into a swirl or marble pattern.

3. Gently push a piece of card stock onto the surface.

4. Carefully remove the card stock by holding one side or a corner. Continue to make more sheets using the same pan, skimming off and disposing the muddy colors. Marbled papers are beautiful when cut and used as a background for a focal point.

TIPS

Either use the paint stick to scrape off the remaining shaving cream, or allow it to turn powdery before buffing it off the paper with a paper towel. When scraping, use sweeping motions to avoid streaks in your design.

Even "muddy-colored" foam can be interesting, spread like icing onto card stock and allowed to air dry.

SLIDER CARD

A card construction technique in which an element is made to move or "slide" on a track or other mechanism, causing another element to be revealed, pop up, or cause movement.

SNAIL MAIL

Mail that is delivered by the traditional postal service, so-called because of the time it takes compared to sending something via e-mail.

SOFT PASTEL

See Pastel.

SOUVENIR

A keepsake that serves as a reminder. Meaning literally the "act of remembering" in French.

This fun, yet romantic card is a lovely reminder of a special dinner at a special restaurant. The heart medallion was a drink stirrer from an anniversary toast. On a card, it becomes a focal point and the sentiment itself—a nice souvenir and a nice memory. The background was created by smudging soft pastels over the background and drawing on a few pink hearts. It was sprayed with fixative before completing the card.

SPATTER

A technique introducing background or foreground color that unifies a composition and provides a textural quality.

HOW-TO BASICS: **SPATTER**

1. Use watercolor markers to stamp onto paper. Use several analogous colors, and spend a few minutes coloring in the design. Dip a brush in water and "wash" the fish, creating even more color.

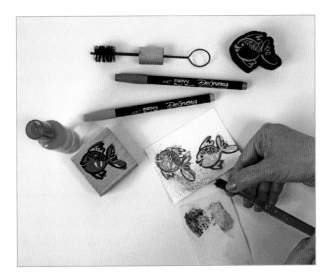

2. Use an old toothbrush or spatter brush, and run a finger toward you over the bristles. This will cause the watercolor to spatter onto the fish. Spatter is a great way to add texture to a smooth surface and subtly create more interest. When complete, cut out the fish and adhere to a colorful background paper.

SPECIALTY PAINT

An art material made of pigment and binder that also contains webbing, glitter, or other special additives. Specialty paints are ideal for card makers because they dry quickly, provide interesting patterns or colors to designs, and are readily available at local craft stores. *See also* Paint.

Webbing spray is a unique paint, coming out of the can in random, colorful, stringy patterns. Compositionally, it can unify card elements, tying together layers and adding texture to the background and foreground. To expand color choices, quickly brayer on metallic foils or dust on mica fragments as the webbing spray is drying.

Another card made with specialty webbing spray paint

SPINNER CARD

A card construction technique featuring a decorative paper element attached to a fine thread. The element is spun around many times until the card is closed, and the card is placed into the envelope. When the recipient opens the card, the element spins, causing a delightful kinetic card.

SPIRELLI

A card making technique using thread, cord, or ribbon to decoratively wrap die-cuts or specially made templates.

SPONGE

An absorbent, porous fiber, either natural or man-made, that can blend color or create textural effects in paper craft.

Load a texturing sponge with paint or ink to create an all-over pattern, taking care to twist the sponge to off-load the paint.

Apply several colors of watercolor markers with a cosmetic sponge. In one sweep, create each letter. Reload the sponge before beginning another letter. Colorful handmade stickers and a brush marker complete this extravagant mail art envelope.

Spray Adhesive

A substance in aerosol form that creates adhesion for photos, illustrations, maps, posters, and signs. This adhesive resists heat and moisture for a strong, permanent bond. Not all sprays are acid free or manufactured specifically for paper crafts. Read the manufacturer's information, and heed all hazard labels on the can. Always work outdoors as the vapors from spray adhesives are harmful. *See also* Adhesive.

Stamp Board

A clay-coated wood stamping surface that you can sand, etch, and stamp. A stamp board accepts all dye-based ink, watercolor markers, and various other coloring agents.

Stamp Cleaner

A tool with an applicator on top used to clean ink from stamps. To clean a stamp, use a gentle motion to apply cleaner, and then pat dry on paper towels.

Stamp Positioner

A two-piece device used for exactly lining up one rubber-stamped image over another. One piece is an acrylic L-shape, and the other a flat square of acrylic or acetate. Uses include: lining up elements such as borders and letters; precise alignment of a stamped image over a previously stamped image; and correcting an incomplete stamped image. *See also* Spritzing.

HOW-TO BASICS:
USING A STAMP POSITIONER

1. Place the L-shaped piece on the table.

2. Seat the acrylic sheet firmly against the two sides of the L.

3. Ink a stamp with pigment ink and fit it firmly against the two sides; then stamp.

4. Move the L away and align the image over the card stock. Place it exactly where you'd like to place the image.

5. Move the L back into place and hold it firmly in place.

6. Move the stamped acrylic away. Fit and stamp the inked stamp into the L's corner, perfectly aligning the image.

TIP

Stamping on thin acetate with permanent ink—saving rather than cleaning off the image—will eventually provide you with a bank of pre-stamped images that are always ready to go.

Stamping

To reproduce the same image multiple times with a hand tool made of rubber, clear polymer, or other material, or a carved eraser or potato. *See also* Bleach, Clear Art Stamp, Foam Stamp, Hand-Carved Stamp, Mounted Stamp, Roller Stamp, Rubber Stamp, Self-Inking Stamp, and Unmounted Stamp.

Stamping Mat

A durable foam work surface for stamping. A mat provides a slight "give," allowing for the best ink impressions, particularly for oversized stamps.

STICKER PAPER

A label stock paper, suitable for printers, laser, stamping, watercolor, and rubber stamping. *See also* Paper and Sticker.

NOTE
No one uses sticker paper like artist Dee Gruenig (page 230). Dee stamps several sheets of the same design at a time, coloring and filing them according to stamp or subject.

TIP
When preparing sticker paper, keep several card elements handy and ready to assemble. Cut them out while you're on the phone or watching TV.

STIPPLING

A method of applying tiny dots of color with the tip of a brush to create a textured effect that simulates a fine, sandy appearance. Also known as pouncing, this technique is also suitable for adding subtle color and glazing.

STREAK

Stamping an image, then dragging the stamp without lifting, in order to create the feeling of movement.

STUDIO PAPER

A special paper that can be printed with an image using a computer and inkjet printer. The image can be transferred onto card stock by rubbing with a tissue or cotton ball. *See also* Transfer.

HOW-TO BASICS:
STUDIO PAPER TRANSFERS

1. Insert the paper into your inkjet printer and print your favorite photo or portrait onto the paper.

TIP
For best results, set the printer on "best" or "photo" so it lays down the maximum amount of ink. If you are printing words, make sure to set the printer on "mirror image."

2. Turn the paper onto card stock and burnish the photo area with a burnishing tool or bone folder. Lift carefully at a corner to check if the transfer is complete. Take your time with this.

3. Lift and wipe the remaining ink off the Studio Paper. You can reuse it many times and on both sides.

4. Trim and use your transfer immediately or manipulate the color using a wet paintbrush.

An image on studio paper can be transferred onto card stock to make numerous cards.

friends forever

STYLUS

In ancient times, a stylus was a pointed writing tool used to inscribe wax or clay. The Sumerians used a wedge-shaped stylus for their cuneiform writing. In the medieval period, a stylus was a pointed writing tool used for ruling a manuscript. Today a stylus is a small hand tool with a blunt rounded end used to emboss or deboss paper.

SWAP

Making multiples of cards, bookmarks, postcards, etc. for the purpose of swapping with others in order to acquire many different cards. When planning a gathering for making swaps, a host or hostess will often select one or two themes that all cards in the swap must follow. It is considered correct to send the swap hostess a card or small gift.

SWIVEL BLADE

See Craft Knife.

TAG ART CARD

A technique using a tag of any size, shape, or weight as a card or a surprise element inside a card.

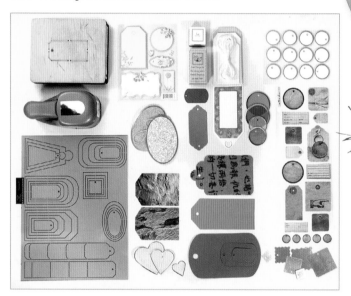

TAPE

A paper, plastic, foam, or foil material with adhesive on one or both sides used to fasten items or in card making techniques. Tape varieties include cellophane, double-sided, dry, mounting, and masking. *See also* Adhesive.

Tape adhesives are the best for fast, convenient card making. From double-sided tape to dry glue tape, dry tapes keep cards flat, neat, and tidy.

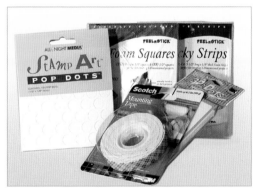

Cards can be just flat pieces of colored paper. But with dimensional tape, you can easily lift up specific design elements to create three-dimensional cards.

1. Tear small pieces of masking tape and overlap them onto card stock, leaving the edges ragged.

2. Sponge watercolor, ink, acrylic, or chalk onto the tape. The result is a highly textured, compositional element that's also the ideal background paper for this card.

Teabag Folding

The technique of folding and cutting teabag-like papers into patterns to create a desired repetitive pattern. *See also* Kaleidoscope Card.

HOW-TO BASICS: **TEABAG FOLDING**

1. Print, stamp, or purchase special papers made especially for this technique.

2. Cut them carefully so they remain identical in size.

3. Begin folding the edges in to form a kite shape. Burnish the edges with a bone folder.

4. Fold all the pieces, and then assemble them using a dry tape.

5. Use a gel pen to create stitching, and embellish the center if desired.

Tearing

Using the torn edge of paper as a textural or color design component in card making.

Tearing aged papers, especially with the image selected here, gives the feeling that this card was recently excavated from an archaeological dig in Australia.

Delicate tearing and pearlescent highlights provide this card with a sweet, vintage sophistication.

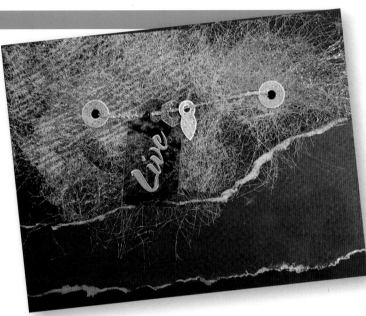

Tearing the paper and highlighting it with a gold marker strengthens the composition. Overlaying the pressed Gossamer fibers adds a stunning finishing touch.

After watercolor painting, stamping, and embossing the black card stock, begin to tear around the image. Hold the image facing you, and tear it away from you, exposing the black of the paper and creating a natural frame around the work. Adding touches of mica and mounting it onto webbing-sprayed card stock produce an organic collage.

TEMPLATE

A thin metal or plastic plate with a cut outline used as a guide in making something repeatedly and accurately that establishes or serves as a pattern. *See also* Stencil.

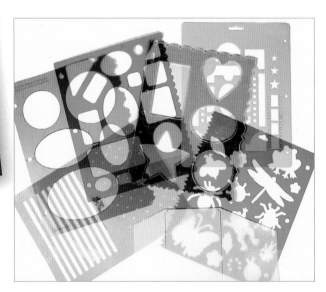

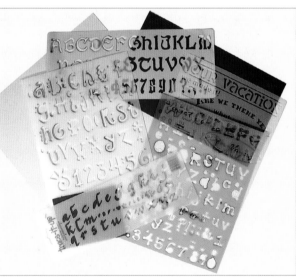

TERTIARY COLOR

See Color.

TEXTILE

Any material relating to fabric or fabric making suitable for use in cards, including ribbon, felt, yarn, fibers, cloth, and leather or leather-like materials.

Jean Harley Shackleford,
Textiles

One part of Jean Harley Shackelford's creative inspiration goes all the way back to an important childhood lesson. "My mother always insisted on the importance of handwritten notes, whether it's a thank you, birthday or how-do-you-do," says Jean, who has a Master of Fine Arts degree from Savannah College of Art and Design.

It's a notion she carried through her education and into adulthood. It's the foundation on which she built a career, going from simply writing notes to making and marketing her own line of greeting cards: Bobbin Designs.

Named for her great-grandmother, Jean's line of cards features charming creatures bedecked in jewels and feathers, quilted, hand-stitched, and otherwise embellished. "Each piece is handcrafted, evoking an optimistic, happy-go-lucky sentiment," she says.

Kate's Paperie in New York City and Gump's in San Francisco carry Jean's cards, which she says are inspired by "random ideas that happen while falling asleep on the train or at some bizarre random moment."

Now, isn't that how everyone creates?

TEXTURE

To impart a desirable surface characteristic or distinctive pattern. In card making, you can create texture by using a variety of paper craft techniques, tools, and materials.

In these three examples, artist cement was used to create a textural, fluffy appearance. Begin by tracing a stencil or stamping an image. Fill it in using the artist cement, a craft stick, and toothpicks. Embellish the card with watercolor, buttons, and chalk once it is dry.

TEXTURE PLATE

A flat sheet of rubber, plastic, or other material used to create textural patterns on surfaces such as paper, clay, and metal.

Condition gold-colored polymer clay, then run it and a texture plate through a pasta machine. When baked, the flat image produces a lovely textural background that may be further manipulated with mica pigments and inks.

Textured card

THANKSGIVING CARD

A card you send to family and friends for the Thanksgiving holiday (celebrated on different days in the U.S. and Canada). You might not think to send a card for this day, but if you can't be there in person, a handmade card is the next best thing. Here are a couple of samples to show you just how. *See also* Holiday Celebration Card.

THANK YOU CARD

This is a card you send to thank someone for a generous gift, a thoughtful gesture, some needed help, or even another card! Thank you cards make up a significant portion of non-holiday cards. Here are some samples to get your mind working. *See also* Special Occasion Card.

THERMO ACETATE

A clear plastic that you can stamp, emboss, or use as a window for a shaker card. Thermo acetate can withstand the heat of embossing.

THERMOGRAPHY

A technique that uses a stamped image, ink, or gilding adhesive with thermal embossing powder to create a raised image when heat is applied. Also known as thermal embossing. *See also* Emboss, Embossing Powder, Heat Embossing.

HOW-TO BASICS: THERMAL EMBOSSING

Materials and Tools
Antistatic pad
Paper
Pigment ink, embossing ink, or gilding adhesive
Rubber stamp(s)
Embossing powder
Scrap paper for collecting the powder
Small dipper or spoon
Heat tool
Soft brush

Instructions
1. Lightly wipe the antistatic pad across the paper to absorb oils, moisture, and static.

2. Apply the ink or gilding adhesive onto an applicator (like a rubber stamp) and transfer that to the working paper surface. How you apply the ink or adhesive may vary depending on your creative objective. Stamps are the most common form of application, but you can also use a brush, brayer, or some other implement. If using a stamp, apply a uniform pressure.

3. Sprinkle a small amount of embossing powder over the stamped image.

4. Tilt the card, allowing the powder to spread across the image and adhere to the wet or tacky areas.

5. Dump the excess powder back into a container, and gently tap the back of the paper, removing tiny embossing particles.

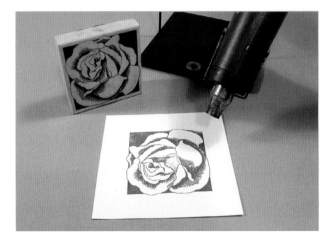

6. Heat the powder until it melts, using a slow, steady sweep and targeting the embossed areas.

7. When cool, use a soft brush to remove any excess antistatic material.

8. You can leave the design as it is or color it with watercolor, pencils, paints, or chalks.

THERMAL EMBOSSING TIPS

- Avoid rocking the stamp, which creates shadow images.

- Work on a padded surface to obtain a good image using less pressure.

- Remember that different papers and inks have varying drying times.

- Drying speed is affected by humidity and the amount of embossing powder you use.

- Don't overheat the embossing powder, which can cause it to lose definition and shape.

- Don't overheat the paper, which can cause it to curl or burn.

A thicker embossing powder provides a raindrop effect, which is especially pretty on a marbled background.

THINKING OF YOU CARD

The only card sent for no other reason than to connect with a friend or loved one. There is no better way to show you care than a handmade card. It'll brighten your day while you make it and their day when they receive it. Here are some samples to get you thinking. *See also Special Occasion Card.*

*Wheresoever you go
go with all your heart*
CONFUCIUS

thinking of you

*Wishing you Blue Skies
and Sunny Days*

A
B
C
D
E
F
G
H
I
J
K
L
M
N
O
P
Q
R
S
T
U
V
W
X
Y
Z

THREE-DIMENSIONAL EFFECT

To add dimension in card making by using small, adhesive-backed foam risers (also known as bumpers), or foam double-stick tape decorative elements, stickers, and embellishments. *See also* Tape.

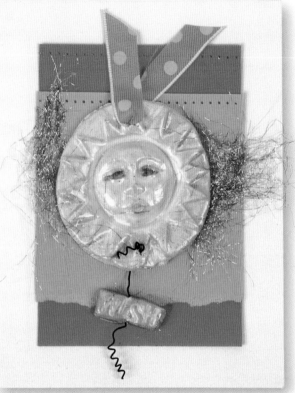

Stamp and emboss an image such as these delicate palm fronds onto a heavyweight card stock. Use detail scissors to carefully cut around the fronds, and then lay them facedown in the palm of your hand. Roll a pencil over the fronds, giving them a delicate curl. Adhere foam risers to the curves, and mount the frond onto a watercolored card. Add mica flakes and bits to achieve a natural landscape.

Air-dry clays offer card makers diversity when creating dimensional cards. Press the clay into a mold, or use a button, cookie cutter, or anything with texture to create a dimensional card focal point.

TISSUE

A soft, thin, usually translucent paper, available in many colors and patterns, used for collaging or as a card insert or overlay. *See also* Paper.

TIP

Select both bleeding or non-bleeding tissue papers, as each performs different tasks. Spritzing or wetting the bleeding type of tissue provides watercolor-like effects. Non-bleeding tissue tolerates a delicate, but wet adhesive.

TOOTH

A slight surface texture caused by the pressure of certain rollers during the paper's manufacturing process. A paper's tooth grabs and holds pastels and chalk.

TRADE CARD

An advertising card issued before 1900 by merchants who gave them away in products or with the purchase of a product. Trade cards were popular before the advent of the postcard, and often were collected and glued into large scrapbooks with other die cuts.

Cards using tissue paper

Trade cards

TRANSFER

To move an image from one place to another. Transfer techniques range from methods that require special chemicals and mediums, to easy processes using inexpensive, non-toxic, readily-available materials. *See also* Inkjet Transfer Paper, Rub-on Transfer, and Studio Paper.

With transfer paper and tools, everyone can create artistic cards.

---

1. Apply a piece of wide shipping cellophane tape onto a photocopied image. Rub it down thoroughly with your thumb.

2. Soak the paper with water, and rub it off with your finger. The transfer will be on the cellophane.

3. Adhere it to the card as is, or trim around the image and use it as a laminate or collage element.

TRANSFORMATION

A card featuring a scene composed of vertical slats. By pulling a tab on the card's side, the slats slide under and over one another to transform into a totally different scene. *See also* Moveable Card.

TRANSLUCENT

A material that transmits light, but causes enough diffusion to prevent perception of distinct images; a state between transparent and opaque.

TRAPEZE STRING ART

The technique of suspending decorative elements, such as die cuts, embellished designs, and small collages, in and on decorative thread.

TRI-FOLD CARD

See Fold-Out Card.

TYPEFACE

The style of typed letters used for the body text of a greeting card.

Card with transferred images

ULTRAVIOLET (UV) LIGHT

Invisible radiation present in sunlight, fluorescent light, and to some degree incandescent light. UV light degrades paper, photographs, inks, and adhesives, so protect your finished cards behind protective glass or in UV-safe archives. *See also* Organization.

UNMOUNTED STAMP

A stamp or die that is not attached to a cushion and wood mount. Since stamps can be an integral part of card making, unmounted stamps offer an inherent benefit: easy storage. Because of their shape and size, hundreds of them can fit in a single photo album. *See also* Stamping.

A stamped card

Unmounted stamps are easy to store. Use a brayer or a flat surface (like a small block of wood or the bottom of a paperweight) to use the stamp.

V

V-MAIL

The unusual and ingenious system for delivering mail from American troops to their homes during World War II. Correspondence was photographed and reduced to thumbnail size onto reels of microfilm. The reels were shipped to receiving stations in the U.S. for developing and printed out on lightweight photo paper. These letter-sheets were reproduced about one-quarter the original size, and the miniature mail was delivered to the addressee. V-mail was composed of a letter that folded into its own envelope.

During wartime, greetings may come in many forms. The author's father penned this Christmas greeting to his family, and it was reproduced into V-mail.

NOTE

According to the National Postal Museum, "V-mail ensured that thousands of tons of shipping space could be reserved for war materials. The 37 mail bags required to carry 150,000 one-page letters could be replaced by a single mail sack. The weight of that same amount of mail was reduced dramatically from 2,575 pounds to a mere 45."

VALENTINE'S DAY CARD

A greeting card exchanged in observance of Valentine's Day, February 14. (Samples presented here for you to jump start your own card.) *See also* Holiday Celebration Card.

Artist and businesswoman Esther Howland (1828–1904) was responsible for popularizing Valentine's Day cards. At the age of 19, she received an ornate English Valentine from a business associate of her father. She then began to create and market her own brand of Valentine's Day greeting cards, employing her friends to build a thriving business, which she eventually sold in 1881. See page 11 for a brief biography.

VICTORIAN

Of or pertaining to Queen Victoria I or the period of her reign from 1837 until her death in 1901. Also, the highly ornamented style of architecture, decor, art, and fashion popular in 19th-century England.

VINTAGE

Characterized by excellence, maturity, and enduring appeal; classic.

A card from circa 1945

May your life with blessings teem
And your cares be but a passing dream

A card from the early 1900s

May the fan of this girl
Cheer your heart and soul

Let it sway and twirl
And make you laugh and roll

③ 1955 H. FISHLOVE & CO.   PRINTED IN CHICAGO U.S.A.

This unusual Christmas greeting card has ooh-la-la appeal when you blow on the feather.

The
FAN
DANCER

Season's
Greetings

You're the One ~~

A card from the early 1930s

A
B
C
D
E
F
G
H
I
J
K
L
M
N
O
P
Q
R
S
T
U
V
W
X
Y
Z

WALNUT INK

Walnut ink crystals and water are mixed to a desired level of darkness, and when applied to the paper cause it to appear instantly aged. Dropping raw crystals directly onto dampened paper creates interesting dappled effects.

Walnut ink: another tool in the card maker's box

WARM COLOR

See Color.

WASH

A layer of color, often uniform in tone, applied across the paper with a brush or sponge. *See also* Color Wash.

WASHI PAPER

A type of paper traditionally made in Japan from the bark or fibers of the kozo or mitsumata shrubs and the gampi tree. Washi paper may also contain hemp, bamboo, straw, and other vegetative material. Also called mulberry or lace paper. *See also* Paper.

TIP

Delicate washi papers appear nearly opaque when layered and gently tacked over an image. An acrylic adhesive, such as PPA, firmly adheres the washi paper to the surface, nearly integrating it with the paper below and leaving the beautiful textural pattern, but very little white color.

WATERBRUSH

See Bleach Waterbrush.

WATERCOLOR

A paint in which water is used as the vehicle for carrying the pigment from the brush to the paper. Quality watercolors are made with pigments, not dyes, making them more lightfast. You can mix watercolor from tubes with those on a palette or in a pan and in conjunction with watercolor markers. You can mix watercolor with gouache to provide a base of color for pastels, pencils, and markers. Good watercolors contain emulsifiers that aid in rewetting and in providing smooth color transitions. *See also* Gouache Watercolor.

Gentle washes, leaving lots of white paper untouched, give an illusion of snow without using white paint. Boldly painted trees and the speedy skier emphasize the real scale of such a vision.

After stamping with permanent ink, spritz water directly onto the watercolor paper. Add touches of paint, manipulating it so that every edge bleeds into the others. To avoid muddying the paint, don't over-manipulate it. If you do, however, blot the paint with a paper towel and try again.

This watercolor technique provides the illusion of a school of fish, emphasizing the one swimming perilously close to the viewer.

Interference watercolors provide the most ethereal and beautiful color on dark card stock. The background paper was stamped simply. The central image was stamped, embossed in black, and painted. This card is suitable for any occasion.

WATERCOLOR

Sparkling watercolors produce amazingly luscious works on dark and light-colored card stocks. To use traditional watercolors on dark paper, mix in some sparkling mica-based paints.

Traditional watercolors produce instant and beautiful results. Notice how the artist edged the card in the same red as the holly berry, providing just the right framing.

▪▪ Artist Profile

Cy Thiewes,
Watercolor Artist

One of the better watercolor artists working in greeting cards today is Cy Thiewes. Having retired at 73, Cy moved to Sun City West, Arizona, where she found a wonderful place to develop her creative endeavors. She was thrilled when someone shared with her that nothing has to go to waste. "In fact," Cy says, "I found that not only was I given permission to tear out the good parts of my old paintings and recycle them into something else, but that it was perfectly acceptable!" For Cy, "Making cards was a result of not wanting to 'waste' my paintings. When you grow up being forever told that there is no such word as can't, it is often a nice surprise to see the result when you just jump in to try something new."

Cy's brilliant use of watercolors, ink, plastic wrap and acrylic paint "waste not" cards are beautiful enough to frame, but made to be given. She is one of those people who joyfully just "jumps in."

WATERCOLOR PAPER

A paper made of any natural fiber, usually cotton. Rag indicates the content of the paper; a rag content of less than 100 percent means that synthetic fibers or wood pulp are a part of the blend.

TIP

Cards are relatively easy to make, but what about matching envelopes? Strathmore is among the manufacturers now giving card makers the option to purchase heavyweight, textured, cold press watercolor cards, which are perfect for any wet media, including marker, acrylic, gouache, and watercolor. The matching envelopes even have a deckle edge.

WATERCOLOR PEN

A plastic-barreled brush that can dispense liquid through a brush tip. The barrel can be refilled with color, bleach, water, or other fluid material.

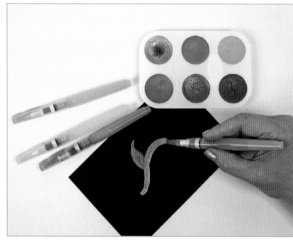

Watercolor pens in action—the color of the pen stock is purely decorative; you can fill a pen with any color.

WATERCOLOR PENCIL

A watercolor paint in a solid form, encased in a pencil. Watercolor pencils may be used independent of water, dipped in water, washed over a watery surface, or used with watercolors themselves.

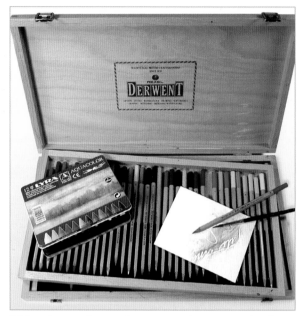

Watercolor pencils come in as many colors as normal watercolor paints. They're easy to blend together, too.

Two watercolored cats cuddle together to view the magnificent skyline created with watercolor pencils. The textural contrast is a nice touch and makes a strong compositional statement.

WATERMARK

A patterned modification made during the formation of a sheet of paper while it is still wet. The pattern, design, or word can be seen in the dried sheet when held up to light.

WATERPROOF OR WATER RESISTANT

A material's ability to resist change when in direct contact with water. This includes, but is not limited to: softening, migration, swelling, bleeding, or dissolving.

WATER SOLUBLE

A material that dissolves in water.

WAX OR OIL PASTEL

See Oil Crayon.

WEAVING

To construct a card or card element by interlacing or interweaving strips or strands of fiber, ribbon, or paper.

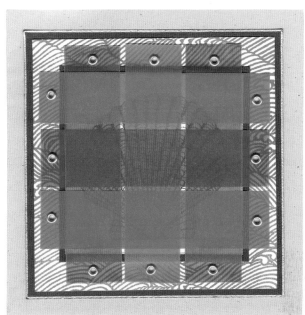

Weaving vellum offers an added bonus. The natural translucency of the material means the colors show through one another, causing a third or fourth color, depending on which one is on top or underneath the other.

Cutting and weaving pretty stamped papers give card artists a myriad of ways to use those scraps. This card is suitable for many occasions.

WEDDING CARD

A card given to a bride and groom on their special day. You can find the sentiments you want to share in a commercial card or you can simply make the card yourself. Maybe it'll touch the new couple so much that your card will end up in their wedding album. *See also* Special Occasion Card.

A B C D E F G H I J K L M N O P Q R S T U V W X Y Z

may your life *together* be full of *love* and your love be full of *life.*

A life of love and laughter... happily ever after...

WET ADHESIVE

Any adhesive that is applied while still in liquid form and dries to a solid to achieve its full bond strength with another material. *See also* Adhesive.

WINDOW CARD

Card stock with a die-cut aperture in nearly any shape, functioning as a window to fill or see through.

Crackled finished paper, stamped and rubbed with glaze, has an old-world appearance. When combined with subtle color and a triple-cut window, it produces a Grecian garden look.

WIRE

A pliable metal strand. Craft wire is usually made of copper and coated with an epoxy colorant. It comes in many gauges or thicknesses, finishes, and colors. Craft-wire tools for card making include rounded-end pliers and wire cutters.

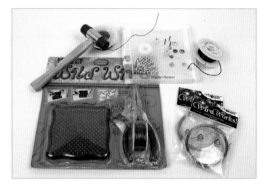

Two wires, threaded with seed beads, appear to hold in place this mica ring, framing a daisy taken from a magazine. To add texture and further interest, mount the entire work on an old piece of repurposed cane.

Create a long, springy coil by wrapping wire around a skewer. Cut the coils to length for arms and legs, and attach them to the snowman that's been stamped, colored, and mounted on foam risers.

WOODCUT

A block of wood on whose surface a design for printing is carved. Also, the print made from a woodcut.

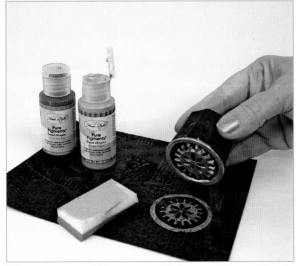

When using a woodblock stamp, it is important to load it well with ink or paint because the wood absorbs some of the pigment. Use a stamping mat to get a stronger image. Woodcut stamps do not deliver the same crisp image as a rubber stamp, but do convey a more naturally hand-made, graphically interesting design element.

WOOD PULP PAPER

A paper manufactured with wood pulp. Wood pulp paper has varying stability due to the variety of lignin contents. Purified wood-pulp paper appears to be as stable as cotton-pulp paper when used for preservation purposes, and it is less expensive. *See also* Paper.

A woodcut card

WRINKLING

A process that creates an aged or distressed look to paper. *See also* Aging and Distressing.

▪▪ HOW-TO BASICS: **WRINKLING PAPER** ▪▪

1. To achieve the effect, crumple dry paper or card stock.

2. Smoothed out the paper slightly by hand.

3. Ink the raised sections of the paper, using a sponge or pigment stamp pad.

4. Spray the paper with a fine mist of water to spread the ink.

5. Dry completely before using. Iron flat on low, dry heat.

A card that uses the wrinkling technique

WRITING CARDS

See Card Submission.

There is a nostalgic quality placed on things that are gently worn. Wrinkling—then using a sponge or pad with ink or glazes to highlight the paper—provides just the right distressing for an aged appearance.

Passover

As you break matzo with those you love,
may you always find peace and hope in your hearts.
Happy Passover

Easter

Easter is one time when it's safe
To put all your eggs in one basket.

Somebunny Loves You!

Just poppin' in
To wish you a hoppy Easter!
Happy Easter

You're wished a basketful of
Bright springtime smiles.
Happy Easter

Rejoice in the Lord!
May all the beauty and glory
Of this blessed season
Fill our hearts with praise.
Happy Easter!

Let us give thanks to the risen
Lord for His glorious gift of life.
Wishing you a Blessed Easter Season.

At this glad time may your heart enjoy a sweet
renewal.
Happy Easter

Earth Day

Celebrating with you!
Sharing the beauty and wonder of our planet.

Come together. Let's share a peaceful world.

Let's reach out to all we know
to make our World more Beautiful.

Cinco de Mayo

Viva Cinco de Mayo!

The years may keep changing
But our Spirit remains the same.
Have a Grand Cinco de Mayo.

MOTHER'S DAY

A mother's duty:
Give your children roots,
Then give them wings.

A Mother holds her children's hands for a while …
And their hearts forever.

God invented mothers because
He couldn't be everywhere.

God made you my Mother …
Love made you my Friend.

House Rules:
#1. Mom's the Boss.
#2. See Rule #1.

Mothers are the roses in the garden of life.

FATHER'S DAY

Anyone can be a dad—
But it takes a man to be a father.

I'm just as lucky as I can be
For the world's best Dad belongs to me.

You're the "bestest" grandpa in the whole wide world!
Happy Father's Day

Thanks for giving me the finer things in life,
your time and your love.
Happy Father's Day

Dad, your life has made such
a wonderful difference in mine!
Happy Father's Day

THANK YOU

I would thank you from the bottom of my heart,
but for you, my heart has no bottom.
—Author Unknown

I can no other answer make,
but, thanks and thanks.
—William Shakespeare

Unselfish and noble actions
are the most radiant pages in the biography of souls.
—David Thomas

Thanks ...
not just for what you did,
but for being you!

Thanks!
I appreciate you!

The smallest act of kindness
is worth more than the grandest intention.
—Oscar Wilde

How beautiful a day can be
When kindness touches it!
—George Elliston

INSPIRATIONAL

There are three sorts of people in the world,
those who can count and those who can't.

Five out of four people can't do fractions.

The farther behind I leave the past,
the closer I am to forging my own character.
—Isabelle Eberhardt

Happiness is not a goal, but a way of life.
—Anonymous

If you don't risk anything, you risk even more.
—Erica Jong

You can only be young once.
But you can always be immature.
—David Barry

BIRTHDAY

May all your birthday dreams come true ... especially the
tall, dark, handsome ones!

This has got to be your best birthday ever!
Just think of all the practice you've had!
Happy Birthday

We heard you were celebrating another birthday ...
Well, maybe celebrating isn't exactly the right word.

May this day be filled with the
warm sunshine of love,
and the bright rainbow colors of laughter.

Happy Birthday.
So many candles ...
... so little cake!

To think of a gift,
I tried really hard.
My mind was a blank,
so I made you a card

Wishing you a birthday filled with dreams
And a year in which they all come true.

A birthday is just the first day of another 365-day
journey around the sun.
Enjoy the trip.

Grandma (or Grandpop)
You're so much fun, it's plain to see,
that while you look grown-up
you're still a kid like me!
Happy Birthday!

Growing old is mandatory;
growing up is optional.
—Chili Davis

Celebrate!
You Deserve the Best Day Ever!
Happy Birthday

Have a Wonderful Birthday, Grandma.
I'm sending special birthday wishes
for a day that's filled with smiles and kisses.

How time flies ...
So sorry I missed your special day.
Happy Belated Birthday

GET WELL

Warning:
The Surgeon General has determined that illness is bad
for your health.
Get Well Soon

After two days in the hospital,
I took a turn for the nurse.
—W.C. Fields

How Do You Mail a Hug?
Get Well Soon

SYMPATHY

You are surrounded by people who love you ...
You are remembered by people who care.
May you find comfort in God's love,
And peace in His faithfulness.
With Deepest Sympathy

Remembering with you
a life so important, to so many.
With Love and Sympathy

May the love of friends and family
be a source of comfort to you at this time.
With Heartfelt Sympathy

Someone so special can never be forgotten.
Thinking of you with heartfelt sympathy.

To live in hearts we leave behind
is not to die.
—Thomas Campbell

And with the morn those angel faces smile
Which, I have loved long since and lost awhile.
—John Henry Newman

For death is no more
than a turning of us over from time to eternity.
—William Penn

RETIREMENT

I'm retired—goodbye tension, hello pension!
—Author Unknown

Golf is played by 20 million mature American men
whose wives think they are out having fun.
—Jim Bishop

The question isn't at what age I want to retire,
it's at what income.
—George Foreman

Rest is not idleness,
and to lie sometimes on the grass under trees
on a summer's day, listening to the murmur of the
water, or watching the clouds float across the sky,
is by no means a waste of time.
—J. Lubbock

Additional Resources

CARD ASSOCIATIONS

UK Greeting Card Association (UK)

www.greetingcardassociation.org.uk

Australian Greeting Card Association (AU)

www.greetingcardassociation.com.au

The Greeting Card Association (US)

www.greetingcard.org

BOOKS ON MAKING CARDS

Each of the following publications from Lark Books and Sterling Publishing contains numerous projects to inspire your own card-making endeavors.

50 Nifty Beaded Cards
Chris Rankin
Paper, 128 pages
Lark Books
ISBN 978-1-60059-146-4

50 Nifty Collage Cards
Peggy Jo Ackley
Paper, 128 pages
Lark Books
ISBN 978-1-60059-121-1

50 Nifty Quilled Cards
Alli Bartkowski
Paper, 128 pages
Lark Books
ISBN 978-1-60059-233-1

Artful Cards
Katherine Duncan Aimone
Paper, 144 pages
Lark Books
ISBN 978-1-60059-140-2

Classic Cards
Marrian Piers
Paper, 160 pages
Sterling Publishing
ISBN 978-1-4027-4739-7

Greeting Cards Galore
Mickey Baskett & Marci Donley
Paper, 128 pages
Sterling Publishing
ISBN 978-1-4027-5376-3

Handmade Greeting Cards for Special Occasions
Amanda Hancocks
Hardcover, 128 pages
Sterling Publishing
ISBN 978-1-4027-4026-8

Teeny Tiny Cards
Jane LaFerla
Hardcover, 128 pages
Lark Books
ISBN 978-1-60059-066-5

Vintage Pop-Up Cards
Taylor Hagerty
Hardcover, 128 pages
Lark Books
ISBN 978-1-60059-031-3

Manufacturers' Materials Reference

7 Gypsies www.sevengypsies.com

Alexx Kesh & Co. www.alexxkesh.com

American Greetings www.americangreetings.com

Art Gone Wild www.agwstamps.com

Art Institute Glitter www.artglitter.com

Artchixstudio.com www.artchixstudio.com

Bazzill www.bazzillbasics.com

Bella Press www.denamidesign.com

Clearsnap www.clearsnap.com

Club Scrap www.clubscrap.com

Comotion www.uptowndesign.com

Craf-t Products www.craf-tproducts.com

Crate Paper www.cratepaper.com

Creating Keepsakes www.creatingkeepsakes.com

DaisyD's www.daisydspaper.com

Delta www.deltacrafts.com

DeNami www.denamidesign.com

Designs By Dreamer www.designsbydreamer.com

EK Success www.eksuccess.com

Fiskars www.fiskars.com

Fragile Crackle www.synta.com/anita1.html

Fred B. Mullet www.fredbmullett.com

Golden Artist Colors www.goldenpaints.com

Hallmark Cards www.hallmark.com

Heidi Swapp www.heidiswapp.com

Heritage Handcrafts www.heritagehandcrafts.com

Home Studio International
    www.homestudiointernational.com

Hot Potatoes www.hotpotatoes.com

House-Mouse Designs www.house-mouse.com

Impression Obsession www.impression-obsession.com

Inkadinkado www.inkadinkado.com

Inque Boutique www.goinque.com

Innovative Stamp Creations
    www.innovativestampcreations.com

It Takes Two www.ittakestwo.com

Jacquard www.jacquardproducts.com

Jolees www.eksuccess.com

Judikins www.judikins.com

K & Company www.kandcompany.com

Ken Brown of Rubber Stamps of America
    www.stampusa.com

Kopp Designs www.koppdesign.com

Krylon www.krylon.com

Magenta www.magentastyle.com

Magic Mesh www.magicmesh.com

Magic Scraps www.magicscraps.com

Making Memories www.makingmemories.com

Marks of Distinction www.marks-of-distinction.com

Marvy www.marvy.com

May Arts www.mayarts.com

McGill www.mcgillinc.com

Me & My Big Ideas www.meandmybigideas.com

Mother Rubberstamps www.motherrubber.com

Mrs. Grossman www.mrsgrossmans.com

Nellie Snellen www.nelliesnellen.com

Offray www.offray.com

Paper Inspirations www.paperinspirations.com

Paper Parachute www.paperparachute.com

Creative Paperclay www.paperclay.com

Pebbles.com www.pebbles.com

Penny Black www.pennyblackinc.com

Polyform www.sculpey.com

Posh Impressions www.poshimpressions.com

Pressed Petals www.pressedpetals.com

Prima www.primamarketinginc.com

Prismacolor www.prismacolor.com

PSX www.sierra-enterprises.com

Quilled Creations www.quilledcreations.com

Ranger www.rangerink.com

Royal Brush www.royalbrush.com

Rubber Stamp Ave. www.rubberstampave.com

Rubber Stampede www.rubberstampede.com

Sandi Miller www.usartquest.com

Savvy www.savvystamps.com

Scenic Route Paper www.scenicroutepaper.com

Spellbinders www.spellbinders.us

Stamp in the Hand www.astampinthehand.com

Stampboard www.stampbord.com

Stampers Anonymous   www.stampersanonymous.com

Stampfrancisco www.stampfrancisco.com

Stamping Sensations stampingsensations.com

Stampscapes www.stampscapes.com

Sunday International www.sundayint.com

The Paper Co. www.papercompany.com

The Paper Cut www.thepapercut.com

Third Coast Rubberstamps www.thirdcoastrs.com

Tombow www.tombowusa.com

Tsukineko www.tsukineko.com

USArtQuest, Inc. www.usartquest.com

Versamark www.tsukineko.com

Woodware Craft Collection www.woodware.co.uk

Wordsworth www.wordsworthstamps.com

Worldwin www.worldwinpapers.com

Wrights www.wrights.com

Zsiage www.zsiage.com

A NOTE ON SUPPLIERS

Usually, you can find the supplies you need for making the projects in Lark books at your local craft supply store, discount mart, home improvement center, or retail shop relevant to the topic of the book. Occasionally, however, you may need to buy materials or tools from specialty suppliers. In order to provide you with the most up-to-date information, we have created a listing of suppliers on our website, which we update on a regular basis. Visit us at www.larkbooks.com, click on "Sources," and then search for the relevant materials. You can also search by book title, vendor, and author name. Additionally, you can search for supply sources located in or near your town by entering your zip code. You will find numerous companies listed, with the web address and/or mailing address and phone number.

Thank you for all you do!

Dear Frankie,
Your friendship means so much to me, more than just a few words here can express, but I'll try.

Thank you, for the enormity of your support in creating so many beautiful cards for this book. Just as importantly, for making sure we ate so well throughout the last several months! You sure are a wonderful cook, a singularly talented artist, and this girl's heartfelt friend.

Thank you from my heart.
Love, Sue

Congratulations!

Dear Julie,
We did it! Congratulations on making it through yet another encyclopedic book. I'll bet you'd never thought we could do it again? It's been so nice working with you and I want to thank you for your thoughtful effort, your time and the talent you've given this project.

You're the best!

Love,
Sue

Your Love fills my Heart

Dearest Dave,
You truly are the most patient soul. Thank you, dearheart, for giving me the time and space I needed to pull this one out. As usual, you've gone over and beyond the call of duty. You're a wonderful man and you have blessed my life.

I love you.
Sue

Artist Credits

Cards on pages 66, 80, 256, and 259 were created with stamps from House-Mouse Designs Inc., P.O. Box 48, Williston, VT 05495. Stamp images © House-Mouse Designs.